CRYPTO MINING IN THE NEW AGE FOR BEGINNERS

A Guide Towards the Opportunities That Cryptocurrency Gives to The Trading World

Table of Contents

INTRODUCTION...6

    Good Reasons to Use Crypto-Currency Bitcoin 7

    How To Do Cloud Mining Using Genesis Mining . 9

CHAPTER ONE..12

WHAT IS CRYPTO MINING?..12

    Bitcoin Basics: What Is Cryptocurrency 14

    Mining? 14

    How Does Bitcoin Mining Work? 15

    How Can You Compete with Millions of 17

    Miners? 17

    Is Bitcoin Mining Sustainable? 18

    What Coin Miners Actually Do 21

    Mining and Bitcoin Circulation 23

    Bitcoin 26

    What Is a "64-Digit Hexadecimal Number"?...........27

    What Are Coin Mining Pools? 29

CHAPTER TWO..31

EVERYTHING YOU NEED TO KNOW ABOUT HOW TO MINE CRYPTOCURRENCY.....................31

    Cryptocurrency Mining 32

    The Best Method to Mine Cryptocurrency 35

    Which Cryptocurrency to Mine? 36

    Best Litecoin Mining Software You Need to Know About 37

    Litecoin mining software - Litecoin charts 38

    Why Should You Care About Litecoin? 38

    Ethereum Cloud Mining – Where to Begin? 43

CHAPTER THREE 51

A BEGINNER'S GUIDE TO CYPTO MINING 51

    Is It Worth It to Mine Cryptocoins? 52

    Mining Pools And Their Share Of Mining 57

CHAPTER FOUR 58

HOW TO MINE BITCOIN 58

    How To Mine Bitcoin 63

    Why do we need mining? 67

    How it works 68

    The future of mining 69

    When is Bitcoin halving happening? 70

CHAPTER FIVE 72

BITCOIN MINING METHODS 72

    Beginner: Using a Bitcoin Mining App 72

    Advanced: Building a Bitcoin Mining Rig 73

    Bitcoin Mining Pros and Cons 74

    Coin Mining: What Is an 'Accepted Share'? 75

How Cryptocoin Mining Works 75
Bitcoin Mining Pools: How To Find and Join 76
One 76
What is a Mining Pool? 77
How You Could Lose Out While Mining 80
Cryptocoins 80
How Do I Reduce These Coin Mining Risks? 81
Cryptocoin Accounts Don't Really Exist 82
What's a Cryptocurrency Wallet? 83
What Are Popular Cryptocoin Account 83
Services? 83
What is a Smart Contract? 84
What Is Bitcoin Cash and How Does It Work? 85
BCH vs BTC 85

CHAPTER SIX 90

IS BITCOIN A STORE OF VALUE? 90

The case for Bitcoin as a store of value 92
The properties of good money 94
The case against Bitcoin as a store of value............ 97
.... 97
Bitcoin as digital cash 97

CHAPTER SEVEN 101

HOW TO BUILD A MINING RIG: THINGS YOU NEED TO KNOW BEFORE YOU START..............101

    Types of Mining Rigs 101

    How to Build a Mining Rig? 103

    The Building Process 106

    The Best Analogy: Google Docs 107

    The Basics of Cryptocurrency Mining 108

CONCLUSION..110

INTRODUCTION

Bitclub Network seems to be the latest in a wave of bitcoin mining income opportunities all around the internet. For a beginner it's hard to discern from the real opportunities and the fake ones. The first thing to know is the fact that crypto-currencies are real and mining them is completely legal and globally practiced business. It is based on computers doing complex mathematical equations to release the next chain of coins into the market. It is completely legal to mine bitcoins all around the world and so are MLM (Multi Level Marketing) companies. The new wave of bitcoin mining income opportunities are mostly a mixture of these two concepts. A clean and professional multi level marketing compensation plan and the unique product of a crypto-currencie mining. Combine these two and you have for the first time on the internet, a truly legal passive income opportunity based on a real product with a real compensation plan. Next time you hear about Bitcoins, Litecoins, Dodgecoins and others and the possible income opportunity, don't be scared, this is just part of the new era of digital currencies and a more computerized world. Everything is going virtual without a doubt. In the past, communication was all about writing and mailing. Today communication is all about writing and e-mailing. The only change is the "e", as in, electronic. Money is no exception. We started to use salt, foods and precious metals as money, later down the road it went to coins, then paper and finally, virtual money. Today we use credit cards, debit cards, echecks, ach and other forms of virtual money. Bitcoins and other crypto-currencies are just an inevitable part of life as we know it. The way our race is evolving has led us to a more comfortable way of using money and that is digital money. So next time you see that opportunity, embrace it. The chances are that you are going to be participating in something that can become the next PayPal or even better, the next United States Dollar.

As for Bitclub Network it is an opportunity to which many are afraid and I understand. We are scared of the unknown and sometimes afraid to try new things. It is only a fact that now over 500,000 people use bitcoin and this number is expected to hit 1,000,000 by the year 2015. So which person are you going to be? The one standing on the sidelines or the one participating and building his own future? The decision is yours to make.

Good Reasons to Use Crypto-Currency Bitcoin

Bitcoin is a comparatively new type of currency that has just started to strike the mainstream markets.

Critics state that using Bitcoins is unsafe because -

- They have no authentic value
- They are not regulated
- They can be used to make illegal transactions
- Still all the major market players talk about Bitcoins. Below are some good reasons why it is worth using this crypto currency.

Quick payments - When payments are made by using banks, the transaction takes some days, similarly wire transfers also take a long time. On the other hand, virtual currency Bitcoin transactions are generally more rapid.

"Zero-confirmation" transactions are instantaneous, where the merchant accepts the risk, which is still not approved by Bitcoin block-chain. If the merchant needs an approval, then the transaction takes 10 minutes. This is much more rapid than any inter-banking transfer.

Inexpensive - Credit or debit card transactions are instant, but you are charged a fee for using this privilege. In the Bitcoin transactions, the fees are usually low, and in some cases, it is free.

No one can take it away - Bitcoin is decentralized, so no central authority can take away percentage from your deposits.

No chargeback - Once you trade Bitcoins, they are gone. You cannot reclaim them without the recipient's consent. Thus, it becomes difficult to commit the chargeback fraud, which is often experienced by people with credit cards.

People purchase goods and if they find it defective, they contact credit cards agency to make a chargeback, effectively reversing the transaction. The credit card company does it and charges you with costly chargeback fee ranging from $5-$15.

Safe personal details - Credit card numbers get stolen during online payments. A Bitcoin transaction does not need any personal details. You will need to combine your private key and the Bitcoin key together to do a transaction.

You just have to ensure that your private key is not accessed by strangers.

It is not inflationary - Federal Reserve prints more dollars, whenever the economy is sputtering. Government injects the new created money into the economy causing a decrease in currency value, thereby triggering inflation. Inflation decreases people's power to buy things because prices of goods increase.

Bitcoins are in limited supply. The system was designed to quit mining more Bitcoins on reaching 21 million. This means that inflation will not be an issue, but deflation will be triggered, where prices of goods will fall.

Semi- anonymous operations - Bitcoin is relatively private, but transparent. The Bitcoin address is revealed at the block-chain. Everyone can look in your wallet, but your name will be invisible.

Easy micro-payments - Bitcoins allows you to make micropayments like 22 cents for free.

Substitute of fiat currencies - Bitcoins are good option to hold national currencies experiencing capital controls, and high inflation.

Bitcoins are getting legitimate - Major institutions like the Bank of England and Fed have decided to take Bitcoins for trading. More and more outlets like Reditt, Pizza chains, WordPress, Baidu, and many other small businesses are now accepting Bitcoin payments. Many binary trading and Forex brokers also allow you to trade with the Bitcoins.

Bitcoin is the pioneer of new crypto-currency era, the technology that gives you a peek into future currency.

How To Do Cloud Mining Using Genesis Mining

Practicing mining these times has become an activity that few can maintain, due to the high costs and maintenance of equipment, along with the payment of associated services of electricity and Internet. That is why this practice has been centralized in few places in the world, where electricity costs are low enough to make mining production profitable. From these difficulties arises what is known as Cloud Mining. Genesis Mining offers legitimate Bitcoin and altcoins mining without hidden charges, in completely transparent transactions, and now they are performing aid conferences to anyone in the Bitcoin community who wants to learn more about the benefits of cryptography. With Genesis Mining, you can mine ETHER, BTC, LTC, DOGE, DASH, BTCD, UNO and assign mining whenever you want, giving all hash power to bitcoins or diversify power in each coin.

1. The first thing to do is open an account at Genesis Mining, it is free, and you can start your investments whenever you want. In the sidebar on the left, we will find all the necessary functions to have full control of our investments. In this step, we will invest by buying mining power, which is basically to buy space on a server and make it work for us. From the menu on the left, select the option "Buy mining power", which will show all the available options to invest. We will not go into detail in each one, as they vary according to the availability of the moment. In this case, we will buy a Bitcoin contract with indefinite duration. We select the amount to invest from the drop down bar, minimum 30 dollars.

3. Now we will choose the payment form (Credit Card, Bitcoin, Dash, Litecoin, Dogecoin) from the panel on the right. This part is essential, so we should pay attention. At the top, we can enter a promotional code to benefit from a discount of 3% on the purchase.

4. In this step, we proceed to make the payment with the chosen method, in this case, Bitcoins. You have 30 minutes to do it, or the order gets cancelled. Below we will see the specifications of the contract, where the most outstanding are the daily maintenance cost and the total BTC we will pay. Finally, we accept the terms and confirm the order.

5. After a few minutes you can go to "My Orders", where you can view the purchased mining contract. From the control panel, we can see that we are already mining Bitcoins in the cloud. Genesis Mining has a fascinating function to distribute the mining power in several cryptocurrencies. For example, with the contract purchased, we can diversify 50% for Bitcoin mining, and the remaining 50% for Litecoin. You can make all the combinations you can think of to maximise your investment.

Final Considerations:

- Mining is a high-risk business and is highly dependent on the price of the cryptocoins.

- It is an attractive opportunity to diversify in the crypto currencies sector.

- Remember to start with a low amount until you understand how the mining business works.

CHAPTER ONE
WHAT IS CRYPTO MINING?

Cryptocurrency mining, or cryptomining, is a process in which transactions for various forms of cryptocurrency are verified and added to the blockchain digital ledger. Also known as cryptocoin mining, altcoin mining, or Bitcoin mining (for the most popular form of cryptocurrency, Bitcoin), cryptocurrency mining has increased both as a topic and activity as cryptocurrency usage itself has grown exponentially in the last few years. Each time a cryptocurrency transaction is made, a cryptocurrency miner is responsible for ensuring the authenticity of information and updating the blockchain with the transaction. The mining process itself involves competing with other cryptominers to solve complicated mathematical problems with cryptographic hash functions that are associated with a block containing the transaction data. The first cryptocurrency miner to crack the code is rewarded by being able to authorize the transaction, and in return for the service provided, cryptominers earn small amounts of cryptocurrency of their own. In order to be competitive with other cryptominers, though, a cryptocurrency miner needs a computer with specialized hardware. Chances are you hear the phrase "bitcoin mining" and your mind begins to wander to the Western fantasy of pickaxes, dirt and striking it rich. As it turns out, that analogy isn't too far off.

Far less glamorous but equally uncertain, bitcoin mining is performed by high-powered computers that solve complex computational math problems (that is, so complex that they cannot be solved by hand, and indeed complicated enough to tax even incredibly powerful computers). The luck and work required by a computer to solve one of these problems is the equivalent of a miner striking gold in the ground — while digging in a sandbox. At the time of writing, the chance of a computer solving one of these problems is about 1 in 13 trillion, but more on that later.

The result of "bitcoin mining" is twofold. First, when computers solve these complex math problems on the Bitcoin network, they produce new bitcoin (when referring to the individual coins themselves, "bitcoin" typically appears without capitalization), not unlike when a mining operation extracts gold from the ground. And second, by solving computational math problems, bitcoin miners make the Bitcoin payment network trustworthy and secure, by verifying its transaction information.

There's a good chance all of that only made so much sense. In order to explain how bitcoin mining works in greater detail, let's begin with a process that's a little bit closer to home: the regulation of printed currency.

Bitcoin Basics: How Bitcoin Differs From Traditional Currencies

Consumers tend to trust printed currencies, at least in the United States. That's because the U.S. dollar is backed by a central bank called the Federal Reserve. In addition to a host of other responsibilities, the Federal Reserve regulates the production of new money, and the federal government prosecutes the use of counterfeit currency.

Even digital payments using the U.S. dollar are backed by a central authority. When you make an online purchase using your debit or credit card, for example, that transaction is processed by a payment processing company such as Mastercard or Visa. In addition to recording your transaction history, those companies verify that transactions are not fraudulent, which is one reason your debit or credit card may be suspended while traveling.

Bitcoin, on the other hand, is not regulated by a central authority. Instead, Bitcoin is backed by millions of computers across the world called "nodes." This network of computers performs the same function as the Federal Reserve, Visa and Mastercard, but with a few key differences. Nodes store information about prior transactions and help to verify their authenticity. Unlike those central authorities, however, Bitcoin nodes are spread out across the world and record transaction data in a public list that can be accessed by anyone, even you.

Bitcoin Basics: What Is Cryptocurrency Mining?

When someone makes a purchase or sale using bitcoin, we call that a "transaction." Transactions made in-store and online are documented by banks, point-of-sale systems, and physical receipts. Bitcoin miners achieve the same effect without these institutions by clumping transactions together in "blocks" and adding them to a public record called the "blockchain." Nodes then maintain records of those blocks so that they can be verified into the future. When bitcoin miners add a new block of transactions to the blockchain, part of their job is to make sure that those transactions are accurate. (More on the magic of how this happens in a second.) In particular, bitcoin miners make sure that bitcoin is not being duplicated, a unique quirk of digital currencies called "double-spending." With printed currencies, duplicating money isn't an issue. Once you spend $20 at the store, that bill is in the clerk's hands. With digital currency, however, it's a different story. Digital information can be reproduced relatively easily, so with Bitcoin and other digital currencies, there is a risk that a spender can make a copy of their bitcoin and send it to another party while still holding onto the original. Let's return to printed currency for a moment and say someone tried to duplicate their $20 bill in order to spend both the original and the counterfeit at a grocery store. If a clerk knew that customers were duplicating money, all they would have to do is look at the bills' serial numbers. If the numbers were identical, the clerk would know the money had been duplicated. This analogy is similar to what a bitcoin miner does when they verify new transactions.

Rewarding Miners
With as many as 500,000 purchases and sales occurring in a single day, however, verifying each of those transactions can be a lot of work for miners, which gets at one other key difference between bitcoin miners and the Federal Reserve, Mastercard or Visa. As compensation for their efforts, miners are awarded bitcoin whenever they add a new block of transactions to the blockchain. The amount of new bitcoin released with each mined block is called the "block reward." The block reward is halved every 210,000 blocks or roughly every 4 years. In 2009, it was 50. In 2013, it was 25, in 2018 it was 12.5, and sometime in the middle of 2020, it will halve to 6.25. At this rate of halving, the total number of bitcoin in circulation will approach a limit of 21 million, making the currency more scarce and valuable over time but also more costly for miners to produce.

How Does Bitcoin Mining Work?

Here's the catch. In order for bitcoin miners to actually earn bitcoin from verifying transactions, two things have to occur. First, they must verify 1 megabyte (MB) worth of transactions, which can theoretically be as small as 1 transaction but are more often several thousand, depending on how much data each transaction stores. This is the easy part.

Second, in order to add a block of transactions to the blockchain, miners must solve a complex computational math problem, also called a "proof of work." What they're actually doing is trying to come up with a 64-digit hexadecimal number, called a "hash," that is less than or equal to the target hash. Basically, a miner's computer spits out hashes at a rate of megahashes per second (MH/s), gigahashes per second (GH/s), or even terahashes per second (TH/s) depending on the unit, guessing all possible 64-digit numbers until they arrive at a solution. In other words, it's a gamble. The difficulty level of the most recent block at the time of writing is more than 13 trillion. That is, the chance of a computer producing a hash below the target is 1 in 13 trillion. To put that in perspective, you are about 44,500 times more likely to win the Powerball jackpot with a single lottery ticket than you are to pick the correct hash on a single try. Fortunately, mining computer systems spit out many, many more hash possibilities than that. Nonetheless, mining for bitcoin requires massive amounts of energy and sophisticated computing rigs, but more about that later as well. The difficulty level is adjusted every 2016 blocks, or roughly every 2 weeks, with the goal of keeping rates of mining constant. That is, the more miners there are competing for a solution, the more difficult the problem will become. The opposite is also true. If computational power is taken off of the network, the difficulty adjusts downward to make mining easier.

Explain it Like I'm Five
Here's a helpful analogy to consider:
"Say I tell three friends that I'm thinking of a number between 1 and 100, and I write that number on a piece of paper and seal it in an envelope. My friends don't have to guess the exact number, they just have to be the first person to guess any number that is less than or equal to the number I am thinking of. And there is no limit to how many

guesses they get. "Let's say I'm thinking of the number 19. If Friend A guesses 21, they lose because 21>19. If Friend B guesses 16 and Friend C guesses 12, then they've both theoretically arrived at viable answers, because 16<19 and 12<19. There is no 'extra credit' for Friend B, even though B's answer was closer to the target answer of 19. "Now imagine that I pose the 'guess what number I'm thinking of' question, but I'm not asking just three friends, and I'm not thinking of a number between 1 and 100. Rather, I'm asking millions of would-be miners and I'm thinking of a 64-digit hexadecimal number. Now you see that it's going to be extremely hard to guess the right answer."

How Can You Compete with Millions of Miners?

If 1 in 13 trillion doesn't sound difficult enough as is, here's the catch to the catch. Not only do bitcoin miners have to come up with the right hash, but they also have to be the first to do it. Because bitcoin mining is essentially guesswork, arriving at the right answer before another miner has almost everything to do with how fast your computer can produce hashes. Just a decade ago, bitcoin mining could be performed competitively on normal desktop computers. Over time, however, miners realized that graphics cards commonly used for video games were more effective and they began to dominate the game. In 2013, bitcoin miners started to use computers designed specifically for mining cryptocurrency as efficiently as possible, called Application-Specific Integrated Circuits (ASIC). These can run from several hundred dollars to tens of thousands but their efficiency in mining Bitcoin is superior. Today, bitcoin mining is so competitive that it can only be done profitably with the most up-to-date ASICs. When using desktop computers, GPUs, or older models of ASICs, the cost of energy consumption actually exceeds the revenue generated. Even with the newest unit at your disposal, one computer is rarely enough to compete with what miners call "mining pools." A mining pool is a group of miners who combine their computing power and split the mined bitcoin between participants. A disproportionately large number of blocks are mined by pools rather than by individual miners. Mining pools and companies have represented large percentages of bitcoin's computing power.

Is Bitcoin Mining Sustainable?

Between 1 in 13 trillion odds, scaling difficulty levels, and the massive network of users verifying transactions, one block of transactions is verified roughly every 10 minutes. But it's important to remember that 10 minutes is a goal, not a rule. The bitcoin network can process about seven transactions per second, with transactions being logged in the blockchain every 10 minutes. For comparison, Visa can process somewhere around 24,000 transactions per second. As the network of bitcoin users continues to grow, however, the number of transactions made in 10 minutes will eventually exceed the number of transactions that can be processed in 10 minutes. At that point, waiting times for transactions will begin and continue to get longer, unless a change is made to the bitcoin protocol. This issue at the heart of the bitcoin protocol is known as "scaling." While bitcoin miners generally agree that something must be done to address scaling, there is less consensus about how to do it. There have been two major solutions proposed to address the scaling problem. Developers have suggested either (1) creating a secondary "off-chain" layer to Bitcoin that would allow for faster transactions that can be verified by the blockchain later, or (2) increasing the number of transactions that each block can store. With less data to verify per block, the Solution 1 would make transactions faster and cheaper for miners. Solution 2 would deal with scaling by allowing for more information to be processed every 10 minutes by increasing block size. In July 2017, bitcoin miners and mining companies representing roughly 80% to 90% of the network's computing power voted to incorporate a program that would decrease the amount of data needed to verify each block. That is, they went with Solution 1. The program that miners voted to add to the bitcoin protocol is called a segregated witness, or SegWit. This term is an amalgamation of Segregated, meaning "to separate," and Witness, which refers to "signatures on a bitcoin transaction." Segregated Witness, then, means to separate transaction signatures from a block — and attach them as an extended block. While adding a single program to the bitcoin protocol may not seem like much in the way of a solution, signature data has been estimated to account for up to 65% of the data processed in each block of transactions. Less than a month later in August 2017, a group of miners and developers initiated a hard fork, leaving the bitcoin network to create a new currency using the same codebase as bitcoin. Although this group agreed with the need for a solution to scaling, they worried that adopting segregated witness technology would not fully address the scaling problem. Instead, they went with Solution 2. The resulting currency, called "bitcoin cash," increased the blocksize to 8 MB in order to accelerate the verification process to allow a performance of around 2 million transactions per day. On November 6, 2019, Bitcoin Cash was valued at about $302 to Bitcoin's roughly $9,330. Cryptocurrency mining is painstaking, costly and only sporadically rewarding. Nonetheless, mining has a magnetic appeal for many investors interested in cryptocurrency because of the fact that miners are rewarded for their work with crypto tokens. This may be because entrepreneurial types see mining as pennies from heaven, like California gold prospectors in 1849. And if you are technologically inclined, why not do it?

However, before you invest the time and equipment, read this explainer to see whether mining is really for you. We will focus primarily on Bitcoin (throughout, we'll use "Bitcoin" when referring to the network or the cryptocurrency as a concept, and "bitcoin" when we're referring to a quantity of individual tokens). The primary draw for many Bitcoin miners is the prospect of being rewarded with valuable bitcoin tokens. That said, you certainly don't have to be a miner to own cryptocurrency tokens. You can also buy cryptocurrencies using fiat currency; you can trade it on an exchange like Bitstamp using another crypto (as an example, using Ethereum or NEO to buy bitcoin); you even can earn it by playing video games or by publishing blog posts on platforms that pay users in cryptocurrency. An example of the latter is Steemit, which is kind of like Medium except that users can reward bloggers by paying them in a proprietary cryptocurrency called STEEM. STEEM can then be traded elsewhere for bitcoin. The bitcoin reward that miners receive is an incentive which motivates people to assist in the primary purpose of mining: to support, legitimize and monitor the Bitcoin network and its blockchain. Because these responsibilities are spread among many users all over the world, bitcoin is said to be a "decentralized" cryptocurrency, or one that does not rely on a central bank or government to oversee its regulation.

KEY TAKEAWAYS
• By mining, you can earn cryptocurrency without having to put down money for it.
• Bitcoin miners receive bitcoin as a reward for completing "blocks" of verified transactions which are added to the blockchain.
• Mining rewards are paid to the miner who discovers a solution to a complex hashing puzzle first, and the probability

that a participant will be the one to discover the solution is related to the portion of the total mining power on the network.
• Double spending is a phenomenon in which a bitcoin user illicitly spends the same tokens twice.
• You need either a GPU (graphics processing unit) or an application-specific integrated circuit (ASIC) in order to set up a mining rig.

What Coin Miners Actually Do

Miners are getting paid for their work as auditors. They are doing the work of verifying previous bitcoin transactions. This convention is meant to keep Bitcoin users honest and was conceived by bitcoin's founder, Satoshi Nakamoto. By verifying transactions, miners are helping to prevent the "double-spending problem."
Double spending is a scenario in which a bitcoin owner illicitly spends the same bitcoin twice. With physical currency, this isn't an issue: once you hand someone a $20 bill to buy a bottle of vodka, you no longer have it, so there's no danger you could use that same $20 bill to buy lotto tickets next door. With digital currency, however, as the Investopedia dictionary explains, "there is a risk that the holder could make a copy of the digital token and send it to a merchant or another party while retaining the original." Let's say you had one legitimate $20 bill and one counterfeit of that same $20. If you were to try to spend both the real bill and the fake one, someone that took the trouble of looking at both of the bills' serial numbers would see that they were the same number, and thus one of them had to be false. What a bitcoin miner does is analogous to that—they check transactions to make sure that users have not illegitimately tried to spend the same bitcoin twice. This isn't a perfect analogy—we'll explain in more detail below.

Once a miner has verified 1 MB (megabyte) worth of bitcoin transactions, known as a "block," that miner is eligible to be rewarded with a quantity of bitcoin (more about the bitcoin reward below as well). The 1 MB limit was set by Satoshi Nakamoto, and is a matter of controversy, as some miners believe the block size should be increased to accommodate more data, which would effectively mean that the bitcoin network could process and verify transactions more quickly. Note that verifying 1 MB worth of transactions makes a coin miner eligible to earn bitcoin—not everyone who verifies transactions will get paid out. 1MB of transactions can theoretically be as small as one transaction (though this is not at all common) or several thousand. It depends on how much data the transactions take up.

"So after all that work of verifying transactions, I might still not get any bitcoin for it?"

That is correct.

To earn bitcoins, you need to meet two conditions. One is a matter of effort; one is a matter of luck.

1) You have to verify ~1MB worth of transactions. This is the easy part.

2) You have to be the first miner to arrive at the right answer to a numeric problem. This process is also known as proof of work.

"What do you mean, 'the right answer to a numeric problem'?"

The good news: No advanced math or computation is involved. You may have heard that miners are solving difficult mathematical problems—that's not exactly true. What they're actually doing is trying to be the first miner to come up with a 64-digit hexadecimal number (a "hash") that is less than or equal to the target hash. It's basically guesswork.

The bad news: It's guesswork, but with the total number of possible guesses for each of these problems being on the order of trillions, it's incredibly arduous work. In order to solve a problem first, miners need a lot of computing power. To mine successfully, you need to have a high "hash rate," which is measured in terms of megahashes per second (MH/s), gigahashes per second (GH/s), and terahashes per second (TH/s).

That is a great many hashes.
If you want to estimate how much bitcoin you could mine with your mining rig's hash rate, the site Cryptocompare offers a helpful calculator.

Mining and Bitcoin Circulation

In addition to lining the pockets of miners and supporting the bitcoin ecosystem, mining serves another vital purpose: It is the only way to release new cryptocurrency into circulation. In other words, miners are basically "minting" currency. For example, as of Nov. 2019, there were around 18 million bitcoins in circulation. Aside from the coins minted via the genesis block (the very first block, which was created by founder Satoshi Nakamoto), every single one of those bitcoin came into being because of miners. In the absence of miners, Bitcoin as a network would still exist and be usable, but there would never be any additional bitcoin. There will eventually come a time when bitcoin mining ends; per the Bitcoin Protocol, the total number of bitcoins will be capped at 21 million. However, because the rate of bitcoin "mined" is reduced over time, the final bitcoin won't be circulated until around the year 2140. Aside from the short-term bitcoin payoff, being a coin miner can give you "voting" power when changes are proposed in the Bitcoin network protocol. In other words, a successful miner has an influence on the decision-making process on such matters as forking.

How Much a Miner Earns

The rewards for bitcoin mining are halved every four years or so. When bitcoin was first mined in 2009, mining one block would earn you 50 BTC. In 2012, this was halved to 25 BTC. By 2016, this was halved again to the current level of 12.5 BTC. In about 2020, the reward size will be halved again to 6.25 BTC. As of the time of writing, the reward for completing a block is 12.5 Bitcoin. In November of 2019, the price of Bitcoin was about $9,300 per bitcoin, which means you'd earn $116,250 (12.5 x 9,300) for completing a block.3 Not a bad incentive to solve that complex hash problem detailed above, it might seem.

Bitcoin Mining Rewards

If you want to keep track of precisely when these halvings will occur, you can consult the Bitcoin Clock, which updates this information in real time. Interestingly, the market price of bitcoin has, throughout its history, tended to correspond closely to the marginal cost of mining a bitcoin.

If you are interested in seeing how many blocks have been mined thus far, there are several sites, including Blockchain.info, that will give you that information in real time.

Equipment Needed to Mine

Although early on in bitcoin's history individuals may have been able to compete for blocks with a regular at-home computer, this is no longer the case. The reason for this is that the difficulty of mining bitcoin changes over time. In order to ensure smooth functioning of the blockchain and its ability to process and verify transaction, the Bitcoin network aims to have one block produced every 10 minutes or so. However, if there are one million mining rigs competing to solve the hash problem, they'll likely reach a solution faster than a scenario in which 10 mining rigs are working on the same problem. For that reason, Bitcoin is designed to evaluate and adjust the difficulty of mining every 2,016 blocks, or roughly every two weeks. When there is more computing power collectively working to mine for bitcoin, the difficulty level of mining increases in order to keep block production at a stable rate. Less computing power means the difficulty level decreases. To get a sense of just how much computing power is involved, when Bitcoin launched in 2009 the initial difficulty level was one. As of Nov. 2019, it is more than 13 trillion.

All of this is to say that, in order to mine competitively, miners must now invest in powerful computer equipment like a GPU (graphics processing unit) or, more realistically, an application-specific integrated circuit (ASIC). These can run from $500 to the tens of thousands. Some miners—particularly Ethereum miners—buy individual graphics cards (GPUs) as a low-cost way to cobble together mining operations. The photo below is a makeshift, home-made mining machine. The graphics cards are those rectangular blocks with whirring circles. Note the sandwich twist-ties holding the graphics cards to the metal pole. This is probably not the most efficient way to mine, and as you can guess, many miners are in it as much for the fun and challenge as for the money.

Bitcoin

The "Explain It Like I'm Five" Version
The ins and outs of bitcoin mining can be difficult to understand as is. Consider this illustrative example for how the hash problem works: I tell three friends that I'm thinking of a number between one and 100, and I write that number on a piece of paper and seal it in an envelope. My friends don't have to guess the exact number; they just have to be the first person to guess any number that is less than or equal to the number I am thinking of. And there is no limit to how many guesses they get. Let's say I'm thinking of the number 19. If Friend A guesses 21, they lose because of 21>19. If Friend B guesses 16 and Friend C guesses 12, then they've both theoretically arrived at viable answers, because of 16<19 and 12<19. There is no "extra credit" for Friend B, even though B's answer was closer to the target answer of 19. Now imagine that I pose the "guess what number I'm thinking of" question, but I'm not asking just three friends, and I'm not thinking of a number between 1 and 100. Rather, I'm asking millions of would-be miners and I'm thinking of a 64-digit hexadecimal number. Now you see that it's going to be extremely hard to guess the right answer. If B and C both answer simultaneously, then the ELI5 analogy breaks down. In Bitcoin terms, simultaneous answers occur frequently, but at the end of the day, there can only be one winning answer. When multiple simultaneous answers are presented that are equal to or less than the target number, the Bitcoin network will decide by a simple majority—51%—which miner to honor. Typically, it is the miner who has done the most work, that s, the one that verifies the most transactions. The losing block then becomes an "orphan block." Orphan blocks are those that are not added to the blockchain. Miners who successfully solve the hash problem but who haven't verified the most transactions are not rewarded with bitcoin.

What Is a "64-Digit Hexadecimal Number"?

Well, here is an example of such a number: 0000000000000000065fcd708cf0130d95e27c5819203e9f964ac56e4df578ce
The number above has 64 digits. Easy enough to understand so far. As you probably noticed, that number consists not just of numbers, but also letters of the alphabet. Why is that? To understand what these letters are doing in the middle of numbers, let's unpack the word "hexadecimal." As you know, we use the "decimal" system, which means it is base 10. This, in turn, means that every digit of a multi-digit number has 10 possibilities, zero through nine. "Hexadecimal," on the other hand, means base 16, as "hex" is derived from the Greek word for six and "deca" is derived from the Greek word for 10. In a hexadecimal system, each digit has 16 possibilities. But our numeric system only offers 10 ways of representing numbers (zero through nine). That's why you have to stick letters in, specifically letters a, b, c, d, e and f. If you are mining bitcoin, you do not need to calculate the total value of that 64-digit number (the hash). I repeat: You do not need to calculate the total value of a hash. So, what do "64-digit hexadecimal numbers" have to do with bitcoin mining? Remember that ELI5 analogy, where I wrote the number 19 on a piece of paper and put it in a sealed envelope? In bitcoin mining terms, that metaphorical undisclosed number in the envelope is called the target hash. What miners are doing with those huge computers and dozens of cooling fans is guessing at the target hash. Miners make these guesses by randomly generating as many "nonces" as possible, as fast as possible. A nonce is short for "number only used once," and the nonce is the key to generating these 64-bit hexadecimal numbers I keep talking about. In Bitcoin mining, a nonce is 32 bits in size—much smaller than the hash, which is 256 bits. The first miner whose nonce gener-

ates a hash that is less than or equal to the target hash is awarded credit for completing that block and is awarded the spoils of 12.5 BTC. In theory, you could achieve the same goal by rolling a 16-sided die 64 times to arrive at random numbers, but why on earth would you want to do that? The nonce that generated the "winning" hash was 731511405. The target hash is shown on top. The term "Relayed by Antpool" refers to the fact that this particular block was completed by AntPool, one of the more successful mining pools (more about mining pools below). As you see here, their contribution to the Bitcoin community is that they confirmed 1768 transactions for this block. If you really want to see all 1768 of those transactions for this block, go to this page and scroll down to the heading "Transactions."

"So how do I guess at the target hash?"
All target hashes begin with zeros—at least eight zeros and up to 63 zeros.

There is no minimum target, but there is a maximum target set by the Bitcoin Protocol. No target can be greater than this number:
00000000fff-
f000000000000000000000000000000000000000000000000
00000
Here are some examples of randomized hashes and the criteria for whether they will lead to success for the miner:
(Note: These are made-up hashes)

"How do I maximize my chances of guessing the target hash before anyone else does?"
You'd have to get a fast mining rig, or, more realistically, join a mining pool—a group of coin miners who combine their computing power and split the mined bitcoin. Mining

pools are comparable to those Powerball clubs whose members buy lottery tickets en masse and agree to share any winnings. A disproportionately large number of blocks are mined by pools rather than by individual miners. In other words, it's literally just a numbers game. You cannot guess the pattern or make a prediction based on previous target hashes. The difficulty level of the most recent block at the time of writing is about 13.69 trillion, meaning that the chance of any given nonce producing a hash below the target is one in 13.69 trillion. Not great odds if you're working on your own, even with a tremendously powerful mining rig.

"How do I decide whether bitcoin will be profitable for me?"
Not only do miners have to factor in the costs associated with expensive equipment necessary to stand a chance of solving a hash problem. They must also consider the significant amount of electrical power mining rigs utilize in generating vast quantities of nonces in search of the solution. All told, bitcoin mining is largely unprofitable for most individual miners as of this writing. The site Cryptocompare offers a helpful calculator that allows you to plug in numbers such as your hash speed and electricity costs to estimate the costs and benefits.

What Are Coin Mining Pools?

Mining rewards are paid to the miner who discovers a solution to the puzzle first, and the probability that a participant will be the one to discover the solution is equal to the portion of the total mining power on the network. Participants with a small percentage of the mining power stand a very small chance of discovering the next block on their own. For instance, a mining card that one could purchase for a couple of thousand dollars would represent less than 0.001% of the network's mining power. With such a small chance at finding the next block, it could be a long time before that miner finds a block, and the difficulty going up makes things even worse. The miner may never recoup their investment. The answer to this problem is mining pools. Mining pools are operated by third parties and coordinate groups of miners. By working together in a pool and sharing the payouts among all participants, miners can get a steady flow of bitcoin starting the day they activate their miner. Statistics on some of the mining pools can be seen on Blockchain.info.

"I've done the math. Forget mining. Is there a less onerous way to profit from cryptocurrencies?"

As mentioned above, the easiest way to acquire bitcoin is to buy it on an exchange like Coinbase.com. Alternately, you can always leverage the "pickaxe strategy." This is based on the old saw that during the 1849 California gold rush, the smart investment was not to pan for gold, but rather to make the pickaxes used for mining. Or, to put it in modern terms, invest in the companies that manufacture those pickaxes. In a cryptocurrency context, the pickaxe equivalent would be a company that manufactures equipment used for Bitcoin mining. You may consider looking into companies that make ASICs equipment or GPUs instead, for example.

CHAPTER TWO
EVERYTHING YOU NEED TO KNOW ABOUT HOW TO MINE CRYPTOCURRENCY

With cryptocurrencies entering the mainstream with a bang, more and more people every single day develop an interest in this new and strange world of blockchain. A lot of these people come to cryptos because they had heard that it's possible to make money from them. If you're one of those people, you're in luck, because today I want to tell you how to mine cryptocurrency. We'll start by covering the term itself – we'll talk about what is cryptocurrency mining and why people bother mining cryptocurrency in the first place. Then I'll tell you about the different ways you can mine cryptocurrency – their pros, their cons and so on. Lastly, we'll talk about some of the more popular coins when it comes to crypto mining.

Understanding Mining
To put it into very simple terms, crypto mining is a process in which a machine performs certain tasks to obtain a little bit of cryptocurrency. This is the biggest TL;DR possible, so let's branch out a bit, shall we? Imagine that you have a machine that mines crypto coins. We'll talk about the specific types of machines later on in the tutorial, but for example's sake, let's just say that it's your own, personal computer and you're trying to figure out how to mine cryptocurrency. Your PC would perform specific tasks that are required to be able to obtain even the slightest amounts of cryptocurrency. These tasks are called "Proof of Work", and they are designed to create a fair playing field for all the different miners out there. The tasks themselves are math equations. The more miners want to mine one, a specific mining pool – the tougher the equations become. This

brings balance to the pool, but it also motivates bigger and stronger machinery usage. Many more subtle factors come into play while the mining process is happening, but the general idea is that if your device contributes to the "mining", you'll get a share of the spoils. That is a very short and simple way of defining what is cryptocurrency mining. Now let's move on to what you came here to see – how to mine cryptocurrency.

Cryptocurrency Mining

There are a few ways you could go about cryptocurrency mining. I'll cover the main ones here, and start from the easiest one – cloud mining.

Method #1 – Cloud Mining
If you're looking for crypto mining ways, cloud mining is probably the most popular way to mine cryptocurrencies without having to lift a finger. Cloud mining is a process where you pay someone (most often it's a big corporation) a specific amount of money and "rent out" their mining machine called a "rig", and the process of mining itself. This rent lasts for an agreed-upon period, through which all of the earnings that the rig makes (minus the electricity and maintenance costs) are transferred to your cryptocurrency wallet.

How to mine cryptocurrency - coins
The people (companies) that offer these cloud mining services usually have huge mining facilities with multiple farms (tens or hundreds of rigs stacked and operating together) at their disposal and know perfectly well how to mine cryptocurrency. Cloud mining has become so popular mainly because it offers the possibility to participate in the world of cryptocurrencies for people who might not have

enough money to buy their rigs or who perhaps simply aren't interested in owning a rig. There are two options of cloud mining – free and paid. Naturally, a lot of people that are looking for ways to mine cryptocurrency would gravitate towards the "free" options, but it does have its drawbacks (very slow mining speeds, extra conditions, etc.). Paid cloud mining usually works like this: You find a cloud mining host online. You check out the plans that the host offers – there are usually four or five of these plans, ranging from the cheapest to the most expensive one; some hosts even offer you the ability to create and customize your cloud mining plan. Once you know what you want, you simply perform the transaction (meaning that you pay the host), register your cryptocurrency wallet code and that is how you make the first steps on how to mine cryptocurrency! Different plans cost different amounts of money and last for a variety of periods. The standard plans can go anywhere from $500 up to $5000, and last from two years to a lifetime. It is usually expected that you'll break even at around the half-a-year – one year mark, and then profit from that point onwards. No one can know for sure, though, because the prices of cryptocurrencies are very volatile and their prices tend to sway by quite a bit.

Method #2 – CPU Mining
CPU mining utilizes processors to mine cryptocurrencies. It used to be a viable option back in the day, but currently, fewer and fewer people choose this method how to mine cryptocurrency daily. There are a couple of reasons why that is. First of all, CPU mining is EXTREMELY slow. You could go on for months without noticing the smallest amount of revenue. It's also usually not worth it – you make very little amounts of money, but you probably spend ten times that amount on electricity and cooling. The problem mitigates itself by a bit if you can find a place that has nice cooling and cheap electricity bills, but that's rarely the

case. So why do people still even use CPU mining, then? Well, basically because anyone with a desktop computer could do it. All you need to be able to mine using the CPU method is just a computer and a couple of programs. It is possible to do it with a laptop, but it is VERY STRONGLY NOT ADVISED. Your laptop will probably fry and overheat in a matter of a couple of hours. The fact that it's so easy to start cryptocurrency mining attracts new CPU miners every day. Some people that are looking for how to mine cryptocurrency don't care about the details – they just want to start the process as soon as possible, and in any way possible.

Method #3 – GPU Mining
GPU mining is probably the most popular and well-known method of mining cryptocurrencies. If you google "cryptocurrency mining", GPU rigs are going to be some of the first things that you'll see. Cloud miners, for example, use GPU rigs for their services. And these guys are professionals that sometimes have hundreds if not thousands of rigs, so they probably know what they're doing, right? GPU mining is very popular because it's both efficient and relatively cheap. Don't get me wrong, the construction of the rig itself tends to be costly – but when it comes to its hash speed and the general workforce, the GPU mining rig is great. GPU rigs utilize graphics cards to mine cryptocurrencies. One standard rig is made out of a processor, a motherboard, cooling, rig frame and – of course – a few (2 – 8) graphics cards. A typical price for a well-performing and nicely built GPU mining rig aims to be around the $3000 price range. It is a hefty investment but will pay off much faster than, let's say, a CPU miner. People looking for ways how to mine cryptocurrency should check them out.

Method #4 – ASIC Mining

ASICs (Application-Specific Integrated Circuits) are special devices that are designed explicitly to perform a single task, which in this case is crypto mining. ASICs are very well known and treasured because they produce insane amounts of cryptocurrency when compared to its competitors' GPU and CPU. But if they are so good, why didn't I mention them sooner? Well, mostly because they're a big subject of controversy. You see, when the ASIC company announced its new version of the machine, the announcement caused an uproar in the cryptocurrency community. Many people have called for an outright ban on these machines. Why? Because ASICS are so powerful, they rob other miners who are using GPU or CPU rigs of the possibility to keep up both in hash speeds and in earnings. Also, ASICS have twisted the economy of certain specific cryptocurrencies – imagine if the majority of earnings would go to one miner with an ASIC farm, what kind of chaos that would ensue.

The Best Method to Mine Cryptocurrency

Now that you have an understanding of how to mine cryptocurrency and about all of the different ways to do it, which one is the best way? The method that suits you the most depends solemnly on a few key details: are you willing to spend some initial money? If so, how much? Do you want to OWN a rig? Do you even want to do it with a rig? These and many more similar questions will determine your best method for mining cryptocurrency. Generally speaking, GPU and cloud mining seems to be the two big options that people love. CPU mining is slow and tedious, while ASIC mining could get very unpredictable, especially as of late. If you want to build your rig, then GPU is the way to go. If you don't want to spend a dime and just get going ASAP, you could give CPU mining a shot. However, if you're willing to risk it and you're not afraid of controversy – ASICs are a great bet. And finally, if you don't want anything to do with neither rigs nor any other type of machinery – cloud mining is your best bet on how to mine cryptocurrency!

Which Cryptocurrency to Mine?

How to mine cryptocurrency – hardware
Your choice of gear should also depend on the type of cryptocurrency mining that you've decided to do. Some of the obvious favorites would be Bitcoin, Ethereum or Dash. Keep in mind, though, that Bitcoin mining is probably the trickiest of them all – since the coin is so popular, there are many miners around the world tuning into the few pools that there are and trying to snatch at least a small bit of Bitcoin. This might result in you waiting for countless hours until the first drops of Bitcoin start coming in. Keeping that in mind, your best bet would probably be to stick with Ethereum or some other less-popular cryptocurrency. Depending on your method of choice, check out the prices, calculate when your return on investment would happen, do some math and you'll figure it out in no time! As you've probably noticed, there are many different ways on how to mine cryptocurrency. These are simply the main methods – if you'd like, you could even forget about mining and jump into Bitcoin faucets – but that's a whole different story for a whole different day. But it's an option! One thing that you should not only remember, but also do right away is to create a cryptocurrency wallet. Decide on the type of cryptocurrency that you want to mine and simply look up the wallet options for that currency. You'll have no problems finding one for coins like Bitcoin, Ethereum or

Litecoin, but if you want to mine the less-known currencies, then you might need to search for a bit until you find a reputable wallet. Getting a secure and reputable wallet is the most important task when you're starting with cryptocurrency mining. Imagine if you'd be mining for a year and all of your savings would be stolen only because you didn't pay enough attention while choosing the wallet and picked a fishy one that got hacked into. If you're serious and are looking for ways on how to mine cryptocurrency, I would suggest buying a hardware wallet – they are the safest and most trustworthy cryptocurrency wallets out there. Well, this is the end of my tutorial on crypto mining. We've covered a few different topics and explored the different varieties of cryptocurrency mining methods. Remember – the method that suits you the most will depend solemnly on what you want and what kind of resources you have, so choose carefully! If you do decide on giving mining a chance, I wish you the best of luck!

Best Litecoin Mining Software You Need to Know About

Bitcoin's great rise into the mainstream opened up the gates for other cryptocurrencies to grow and expand. Many of these cryptocurrencies have already made some sort of a name for themselves. A lot of people appreciate these so-called altcoins for their mining and trading value. One of the more popular of such altcoins is called Litecoin, and today I would like to tell you about all the different Litecoin mining software options. In this tutorial, we'll cover some of the basic information first (basically, what Litecoin is and why you should care) and then move on to the different Litecoin miner software (Easy Miner, Gui Miner, etc.). We'll talk about the pros and cons of this software, how to use them, and at the very end will try to figure out the best Litecoin miner software there is. Also, I'll share a few tips on how you could pick software that suits you the most.

Explaining Litecoin
In its simplest form, Litecoin is an almost identical spin-off of Bitcoin (at least technically speaking). It was one of the earliest altcoins, coming into existence in mid-2011. The coin was created by a certain ex-Google employee named Charlie Lee. He created the cryptocurrency as an open-source project so that it could be decentralized and independent.

Litecoin mining software - Litecoin charts

Today Litecoin holds the 7th place in the market position and as of the time of writing this article is valued at about $55. It reached this price point after the great crash of crypto prices back at the beginning of 2018.

Why Should You Care About Litecoin?

From the graph above we can see that Litecoin is indeed one of the more active altcoins in the industry. However, why should anyone care about it when there are crypto stars like Bitcoin and Ethereum? Well, first of all, Litecoin is considered to be Bitcoin's biggest rival. Why? Mainly because it has almost identical features and can perform similar tasks – only a lot faster. Currently, in the market, there are four times more Litecoins than Bitcoins. This, in turn, leads to Litecoin being four times faster than Bitcoin. If you're an average person looking to only make transactions and not delve into anything else, then Litecoin is heavily superior to Ethereum in this topic. They do kind of look almost the same at first glance, but Ethereum is great for creating contracts and doing similar tasks, while Litecoin is the coin to go to when thinking about trading and other various transactions.

Litecoin Mining Software
As with a lot of other cryptocurrencies, Litecoin has quite a few mining software. These differ in many aspects starting from their mining speed and ending with security measures. I'm going to list and overview some of the best or most well-known Litecoin mining software. These aren't arranged in any particular order.

Easy Miner
Easy Miner is a well-known and appreciated Litecoin mining software in the cryptocurrency community. It is an open-source (meaning that you can customize it all you want) and free – there's no entry fee to start using Easy Miner. Easy Miner features an interactive and easy to use control panel and offers real-time statistics. It allows you to check the hash rates, shares, and other similar information at any given time. What's super cool about Easy Miner (as a Litecoin miner software) is that it has an inbuilt, custom wallet and extensive online chat and support. This makes the Litecoin mining process *that* much easier and more fun to use. Easy Miner has built a reputation of a trustworthy and likable Litecoin miner software, so if you're looking for a software to start mining, definitely check Easy Miner out.

MultiMiner
MultiMiner isn't as well-known or widely accepted as our previous entry, but it is quite versatile in the way it allows you to switch individual devices while maintaining the ability to manage any mining appliances within your network. To give you an example, imagine that you wanted to switch

from a CPU mining rig to a GPU powered one – MultiMiner will maintain all personalization you've done up to that point in a separate, dedicated network. MultiMiner might not be as intuitive or well optimized when compared to other Litecoin mining software in the world, but it's quite apparent that a lot of work and dedication has gone into building this software. If you'd like to try it out yourself, don't hesitate and go for it!

GUIMiner Scrypt
GUIMiner Scrypt is a fork of GUIMiner. This fork was specifically designed with beginner miners in mind to make the process of starting in cryptocurrency mining more simple and easier to approach. GUIMiner is a CPU/GPU Bitcoin miner designed for Microsoft Windows operating systems. The GUIMiner Scrypt fork was created to support scrypt mining, i.e. Litecoin, Dogecoin, etc. The GUIMiner Scrypt interface is simple and easy to use. It might not be the most aesthetically pleasing software out there, sure. However, it does its job not only in being a good Litecoin mining software but also in being a good gateway for beginner miners.

CPUminer
As the name probably suggests, this is a CPU-exclusive miner. It is a decent Litecoin mining software, except that it might be a bit difficult to understand and get around in if you're an absolute beginner in the field of crypto mining. The CPUminer has received a few updates since its release, one of them being a hashing speed upgrade. Users report being able to perform the same hashing tasks at twice the speed (with little changes on the resource consumption), which is great for anyone trying to find the best Litecoin miner software! CPUminer is available on Windows, Linux and Mac OS, which makes it a viable option if you're

struggling to find a decent mining program for your operating system.

CGminer Litecoin
If you're looking for Litecoin mining software, CGminer Litecoin might be a good choice. It's one of the more popular miners in the market, even though there's not much information regarding its functions online. When searching for CGminer Litecoin, the best place to start would probably be bitcointalk.org forums – there's a thread with all of the available information and a download link provided. CGminer Litecoin is openly sourced, which means that you can add or configure any options that you might want or need.

Awesome Miner
Awesome miner is a less known Litecoin mining software than the others on this list, but it might also be a decent choice. This software has a user-friendly interface and is comparatively easy to use and get around.

Litecoin mining software
The Awesome Miner offers multiple mining engines, a variety of mining pools to choose from, an ability to switch between web and mobile interfaces, various informative notifications, etc. This Litecoin mining software is quite extensive and well-developed, and the ability to switch between interfaces in an optimized, fluid way is a nice bonus.

How to Pick the Right Software?
It's no secret that there is a lot of Litecoin mining software in the market. This list touched on just a few, more notable ones – with a little bit of searching you could find double or triple the amount that is covered here.

So how do you choose when you have so many options? Well, while looking for the best Litecoin miner software, you should keep a couple of things in mind: Interface. You're probably thinking about mining Litecoin for longer than a day or two. Looking long-term, one of the important aspects of any good Litecoin mining software is a welcoming interface. You probably wouldn't want to spend countless hours looking at a clunky and confusing dashboard trying to figure out where things are. Security. Security should be the top priority when trying to find a Litecoin mining software. A program might have a flashy and gamified HUD, top mining and hashing speeds, constant customer support and be free – at the end of the day, if it's hacked and all of your earnings are stolen, what difference does it make? Support. Customer support is also important. What if you run into a bug or a problem that you just aren't able to solve? Sure, you could spend hours on end trying to find a solution on online forums and YouTube videos, but it's much nicer to be able to get help with just a click of a button. Mining speed/hash rate. If a Litecoin mining software takes three years to mine a single coin, that might be a good indicator that it isn't well optimized and you should probably be looking somewhere else. Updates. Finally, good Litecoin mining software will have an extensive log of constant updates and improvements to its various aspects. Whether its an update of some technical parameters or a visual haul – it's always nice to see that the mining program is actively being taken care of. These are just a few key points that you should consider when choosing a Litecoin mining software. There are plenty of other factors to consider (wallet support, different operating system optimization, and availability, payout systems, etc.). The above-listed ones, however, are a good place to start.

I've Got My Software – Now What?

So – after spending what seemed like months searching for the perfect Litecoin mining software, you finally have it installed and are ready to dive straight into the mining. From this point onwards, the process should be smooth and without too many hurdles. Most software will work by themselves without a need for any additional interference on your part. It would probably be a good idea to keep an eye on your software, though. Study how it operates, try out different functions. If the mining program is openly sourced (and most of them are) you have all of the options in the world to customize and experiment with it as much as you like. Also, keep an eye out for updates, changes, improvements, etc. It's beneficial to know what (and why) is happening with your software. Maybe something bugged out completely and it would be a good time to search for a new Litecoin mining software?

Ethereum Cloud Mining – Where to Begin?

Cryptocurrencies are gaining more and more recognition as time goes on. People are starting to use a lot of new terms related to cryptos. "Hashing", "HODLing" and "mining pool" are just to name a few – and most of them revolve around profiting from cryptocurrencies. However, today we're interested in only one specific term – Ethereum cloud mining. In this guide, we'll discuss all Ethereum cloud mining – what it is, why people do it and how to do it. I'll tell you all about the many different options to choose from when thinking about joining the cloud mining business. Furthermore, I'll walk you through the process of establishing your first cloud mining gig and what to do afterward.

Cloud Mining
To put it into very simple terms, cloud mining is a process where you pay somebody to "rent" out their cryptocurrency mining devices, electricity and – naturally – the service of mining itself. People (though more often it's companies) who offer Ethereum cloud mining services usually have huge farms at their disposal. A farm is simply a big amount of mining rigs operating in one specific facility. This facility has to be well equipped, though – cooling has to be up to par, it has to have a lot of space to store all of the mining rigs. A need for huge amounts of electricity is also a thing to consider. If, for example, you'd want to start cloud mining Ethereum, the first thing that you would have to do is to find a host – somebody that would be willing to sell you their Ethereum cloud mining services. After that you would simply agree upon a contract, shake hands (whether physically or via the internet) and that's it! Hosts usually offer a wide variety of available contracts ranging from "minor investment – minor profit" to "huge investment – major profit". People who have never had any experience with cryptocurrencies tend to start from the lower levels of investment. When you see that the service is actually legit and you're slowly but surely making a profit, you can upgrade your contract at any given time. Alternatively, you might want to find a free Ethereum cloud mining host. This, naturally, has its pros and cons, so let's tackle the matter straight away.

Free Ethereum Cloud Mining
As I've mentioned earlier, one of the ways you can start with cloud mining is to find a free Ethereum cloud mining service. In this context, "free" means that you won't have to pay any initial fees to your host, which would usually be the case. You can choose to upgrade your plan if you want to. However, if that is out of consideration, then no initial deposit is required. So how do these cloud mining hosts

profit, then? Well, first of all, people often tend to upgrade to higher profit providing plans. This brings better results, but in turn, has an adequate fee. If you don't want to upgrade to a better plan then the host will simply take a small percentage of your earnings as "rent money" at the end of each month. With that being said, let's look over some of the most popular free Ethereum cloud mining service providers. The list isn't ranked in any particular order.

Swiss Gold Global

Swiss Gold Global (from this point onward: SGG) has been active for around ten years now. They have established themselves a reputation of a professional, honorable and legit company and offer a variety of coins – including Ethereum – to mine.

Ethereum cloud mining - Swiss gold global

SGG offers daily payouts and a secure platform to mine from. In total, they have four different levels of cloud mining (excluding the free one) which range from $249 to $5000. The company also has an affiliate program. One of the best features of the program for people interested in cloud mining is that you can convert your affiliate commissions into a lifetime (yes, LIFETIME) cloud mining contracts. This is such a rare feature that it almost sounds too good to be true. SGG also offers full support on all topics related to cloud mining. Furthermore, they have a feature that lets you sell back your earnings and stop the contract at any given time if you'd only wish. Swiss Gold Global is truly a part of the leaders when it comes to free Ethereum cloud mining. With almost a decade of experience, this company might be worth checking out if you're interested in cloud mining in general.

Nice-Miner

Nice-Miner is another alternative if you're looking for a free Ethereum cloud mining service. These guys let you start cloud mining without a need for any hardware.

Ethereum cloud mining - Why choose nice-miner?

Nice-Miner offers a free registration bonus and a fast responding support service. They also have an affiliate (referral) program, the same as Swiss Gold Global. Nice-Miner's affiliate bonus can stack up to 15%. Nice-Miner lets you choose from three different levels – 3 months, 5 years and a lifetime package. These levels vary in cost but are relatively affordable when compared to other Ethereum cloud mining services in the industry.

Ethereum Miner (ethrun.net)

Ethereum Miner is a user-friendly and well-optimized Ethereum cloud mining host. They offer you a quick setup and a wide variety of plans to choose from if you're interested.

Ethereum cloud mining - ETH miner plans

Ethereum Miner's prices for plans range from 0,5 ETH up to 10 ETH. They are transparent with their services and even provide suggestions on where you could create an Ethereum wallet if you don't have one, and where to buy Ethereum from. According to their official site, you could earn up to 0,0035 ETH per day if you chose to not buy any of their suggested plans and simply mine ETH for free. Keeping in mind the fact that this requires no investment on your part, it's not that bad of a deal.

Paid Cloud Mining
Now that I've covered some of the more popular free Ethereum cloud mining sites and companies we can move on and talk about hosts that require an initial fee for their cloud mining services. It makes sense that free cloud mining is much more attractive than one that you have to pay for out of your pocket, but it isn't just black and white. Even though the above-listed sites offer a service without an initial fee, the mining and hashing speeds are that much slower than those of paid cloud mining hosts. In addition to speed, free Ethereum cloud mining sites rarely give you some or any control of the matter, where Ethereum cloud mining companies that require some sort of an up-front payment are often another story. These hosts, for example, might have cameras installed in their farms and let the customers tune in at any given time via the internet to check on how their rigs are doing. Now you know the pros and cons of free and paid Ethereum cloud mining services. Let's review a list of some of the more popular and established hosts that are known for cloud mining Ethereum. They're not listed in any particular order.

Genesis Mining
The Genesis cryptocurrency mining company is probably one of the most well-known and reputable cloud mining service providers out there. They are widely accepted as the biggest and best-developed company in the crypto mining world.

Ethereum cloud mining - Genesis mining
Genesis offers its customers state-of-the-art mining rigs. They are designed to mine Bitcoin and a variety of other altcoins. The company proudly states that they are an actual, real-world based team of professionals and crypto enthusiasts. Genesis Mining offers the customers four different plans to choose from when it comes to Ethereum

cloud mining, the fourth plan providing the ability to customize the rates in ways that suit you the most.

Ethereum cloud mining prices
The prices for Genesis plans vary, but it is safe to say that you get what you paid for. With ambitious future products, quality ensuring and an around-the-clock working team, Genesis Mining has built the reputation of a trustworthy, achievement orientated company. If you're planning on investing in Ethereum cloud mining, these guys should pop up on your radar.

HashFlare
HashFlare is another recognizable name in the cryptocurrency mining world. The site's default offer is Bitcoin cloud mining, but you also can mine Litecoin, Dash, Zcash and – of course – Ethereum. They require no maintenance fee and use standard GPU mining rigs for their cloud mining processes. What's nice about HashFlare is that they offer detailed statistical information on their site, so you can not only access the info but also analyze and make your mind on the validity of their services. Furthermore, the company lets you choose the mining pool that best fits your needs – this is a great feature for it furthers the freedom that you as a customer have when it comes to taking things into your own hands. Fixed fees, instant withdrawal options, immediate connection – HashFlare has everything that any company would need for cloud mining Ethereum. If you're in search of a decent Ethereum cloud mining service, give these guys a shot!

HashGains
With a similar name to its competitor, HashGains is also a popular choice for people who would like to enter the cryptocurrency mining game.

Ethereum cloud mining - Hashgains prices
HashGains have five different options to choose from when it comes to Ethereum cloud mining (the fifth one being a custom choice). What's nice about this service provider is that they have a fun and interactive interface. People seem to like that. HashGains also proudly exclaim that they have cutting-edge technology hardware, exceptional performance standards, and an ever-ready power backup system. The payout on hash rates and have competitive prices, so be sure to check them out!

I've Got My Ethereum – What Now?
So you chose a cloud mining service provider and have already begun making gains. Cool! The next logical step would be to sell what you've gathered. Many different online merchants are dealing with cryptocurrency sales. The good thing is that you're trying to sell Ethereum – it is huge and popular crypto, you shouldn't come across any difficulties finding someone to sell it to. Always pick a merchant that has a good reputation, is well-known in the community and places security as their number one priority. After you've picked, double-check online – just to be sure. After this point, you're probably good. A lot of the online crypto trading sites have extensive guides on how to register and start trading different cryptocurrencies. At this point, you should have managed to form a general idea on the different Litecoin mining software and their pros and cons. If some of them stood out for you – great! That means that you're probably already decided and know what you want from a cryptocurrency mining software. But there are a few things you should keep in mind before picking one and

sticking with it. Before deciding on software, give it some time. Read the changelogs, forums, talk to people that have used or still use the software that you're thinking about downloading. In this case, third-party opinions and constructive input might be the things that make it or break it for you when it comes to the actual decision making. People are usually keen on helping, so don't hesitate to ask! One good rule of thumb when feeling indecisive about software is to pay attention to its security. If a mining software looks awesome, works intuitively and has all the functions that you could ever need but you're still not sure, check out how it handles and deals with security. That should always be the point that you pay the most attention to. Another thing that you could look for in software is if it supports multiple cryptocurrencies and altcoin mining. The coin that you're mining might take a heavy hit in price (or you might simply want to switch your mining options), so it's a good idea to think two or three steps ahead and plan accordingly. Most of the Litecoin mining software supports other coin mining, too. Remember, though, that you aren't tied to a single piece of Litecoin mining software for the rest of your life. If you don't like something about the program that you're using, you can always throw it out of the Window (see what I did there?) and simply find a new one.

CHAPTER THREE
A BEGINNER'S GUIDE TO CYPTO MINING

Mining cryptocoins is an arms race that rewards early adopters. Bitcoin, the first decentralized cryptocurrency, released in early 2009. Similar digital currencies have crept into the worldwide market since then, including a spin-off from Bitcoin called Bitcoin Cash. If you had started mining Bitcoins back in 2009, you could have earned thousands of dollars by now. At the same time, there are plenty of ways you could have lost money, too. Bitcoins are not a good choice for beginning miners who work on a small scale. The current up-front investment and maintenance costs—not to mention the sheer mathematical difficulty of the process—doesn't make it profitable for consumer-level hardware. Today, Bitcoin mining is reserved for large-scale operations only. Litecoins, Dogecoins, and Feathercoins, on the other hand, are three Scrypt-based cryptocurrencies that are the best cost-benefit for beginners. Dogecoins and Feathercoins would yield slightly less profit with the same mining hardware but are becoming more popular daily. Peercoins, too, can also be a reasonably decent return on your investment of time and energy. As more people join the cryptocoin rush, your choice could get more difficult to mine because more expensive hardware will be required to discover coins. You will be forced to either invest heavily if you want to stay mining that coin, or you will want to take your earnings and switch to an easier cryptocoin. Understanding the top 3 bitcoin mining methods is probably where you need to begin; this article focuses on mining "scrypt" coins. Also, be sure you are in a country where bitcoins and bitcoin mining is legal.

Is It Worth It to Mine Cryptocoins?

As a hobby venture, cryptocoin mining can generate a small income of perhaps a dollar or two per day. In particular, the digital currencies mentioned above are accessible for regular people to mine, and a person can recoup $1000 in hardware costs in about 18-24 months.

As a second income, cryptocoin mining is not a reliable way to make substantial money for most people. The profit from mining cryptocoins only becomes significant when someone is willing to invest $3000 to $5000 in up-front hardware costs, at which time you could potentially earn $50 per day or more.

Set Reasonable Expectations

If your objective is to earn substantial money as a second income, then you are better off purchasing cryptocoins with cash instead of mining them, and then tucking them away in the hopes that they will jump in value like gold or silver bullion. If your objective is to make a few digital bucks and spend them somehow, then you just might have a slow way to do that with mining.

Smart miners keep electricity costs to under $0.11 per kilowatt-hour; mining with 4 GPU video cards can net you around $8.00 to $10.00 per day (depending upon the cryptocurrency you choose), or around $250-$300 per month.

The two catches are:

1. The up-front investment in purchasing 4 ASIC processors or 4 AMD Radeon graphic processing units
2. The market value of cryptocoins

Now, there is a small chance that your chosen digital currency will jump in value alongside Bitcoin at some point. Then, possibly, you could find yourself sitting on thousands of dollars in cryptocoins. The emphasis here is on "small chance," with small meaning "slightly better than winning the lottery."

If you do decide to try cryptocoin mining, proceed as a hobby with a small income return. Think of it as "gathering gold dust" instead of collecting actual gold nuggets. And always, always, do your research to avoid a scam currency.

How Cryptocoin Mining Works

The focus of mining is to accomplish three things:

• Provide bookkeeping services to the coin network. Mining is essentially 24/7 computer accounting called "verifying transactions."

• Get paid a small reward for your accounting services by receiving fractions of coins every couple of days.

• Keep your personal costs down, including electricity and hardware. The Laundry List: What You Will Need to Mine Cryptocoins

You need eight things to mine Litecoins, Dogecoins, or Feathercoins.

1. A free private database called a coin wallet. It's a password-protected container that stores your earnings and keeps a network-wide ledger of transactions.

2. A free mining software package, like this one from AMD, typically made up of cgminer and stratum.

3. A membership in an online mining pool, which is a community of miners who combine their computers to increase profitability and income stability.

4. Membership at an online currency exchange, where you can exchange your virtual coins for conventional cash, and vice versa.

5. A reliable full-time internet connection, ideally 2 megabits per second or faster.

6. A desktop or custom-built computer designed for mining. You may use your current computer to start, but you won't be able to use the computer while the miner is running. A separate dedicated computer is ideal. Do not use a

laptop, gaming console or handheld device to mine. These devices just are not effective enough to generate income.

7. An ATI graphics processing unit (GPU) or a specialized processing device called a mining ASIC chip. The cost will be anywhere from $90 used to $3000 new for each GPU or ASIC chip. The GPU or ASIC will be the workhorse of providing the accounting services and mining work.

8. A house fan to blow cool air across your mining computer. Mining generates substantial heat, and cooling the hardware is critical for your success.

You absolutely need a strong appetite of personal curiosity for reading and constant learning, as there are ongoing technology changes and new techniques for optimizing coin mining results. The most successful coin miners spend hours every week studying the best ways to adjust and improve their coin mining performance. Cryptocurrency, as the name suggests, is a form of digital money designed to be secure and anonymous in most cases. It uses a technique called cryptography — a process used to convert legible information into an almost uncrackable code, to help track purchases and transfers. Giving a simple definition, Blockgeeks says it is just limited entries in a database no one can change without fulfilling specific conditions. Cryptography is a technique that uses elements of mathematical theory and computer science and was evolved during the World War II to securely transfer data and information. Currently, it is used to secure communications, information and money online. Cryptocurrencies allow users to make secure payments, without having to go through banks. Some cryptocurrencies include bitcoin, Bitcoin Cash, Ethereum, DigitalNote, LiteCoin and PotCoin. Bitcoin has the distinction of being the first cryptocurrency, having been introduced in 2009. Since then, this class of cryptocurrencies mushroomed, with more than 900 currently active. How Cryptocurrencies Work. A cryptocurrency runs on a blockchain, which is a shared ledger or document duplicated several times across a network of computers. The updated document is distributed and made available to all holders of the cryptocurrency.

Every single transaction made and the ownership of every single cryptocurrency in circulation is recorded in the blockchain. The blockchain is run by miners, who use powerful computers that tally the transactions. Their function is to update each time a transaction is made and also ensure the authenticity of information, thereby ascertaining that each transaction is secure and is processed properly and safely. As payment for their services, miners are paid physically minted cryptocurrency as fees by vendors or merchants of each transaction. The value of the cryptocurrency fluctuates based on demand and supply, although there is no fixed value for it. Buyers and sellers agree on a value, which is fair and is based on the value of the cryptocurrency trading elsewhere. Since there is no intermediary like bank involved in the transaction, as it is a peer-to-peer transaction, the transaction fee that is associated with credit cards is eliminated. The identity of the buyer and seller are not revealed. However, each and every transaction is made public to all the people in the blockchain network. One can acquire a cryptocurrency through exchanges found online or trade it for traditional currencies. Assume X wants to buy an item valued at $10,000 and he realizes that the seller Y accepts cryptocurrency, say bitcoin, as a form of payment. X scouts around to find the prevailing exchange rate, say $1,000 per currency. X gets Y's public Bitcoin address from Y's website, although both parties remain anonymous to each other. X can now instruct his Bitcoin client or the software installed on his computer to transfer 10 bitcoins from his wallet to Y's address. X's Bitcoin client will electronically sign the transaction request with his private key known only to him. X's public key, which is a public information, can be used for verifying the information. When X's transaction is broadcast to the Bitcoin network, it would be verified in a few minutes by miners. The 10 bitcoins will now be transferred to Y's address.

Mining

Cryptocurrency mining includes two functions, namely: adding transactions to the blockchain (securing and verifying) and also releasing new currency. Individual blocks added by miners should contain a proof-of-work, or PoW. Mining needs a computer and a special program, which helps miners compete with their peers in solving complicated mathematical problems. This would need huge computer resources. In regular intervals, miners would attempt to solve a block having the transaction data using cryptographic hash functions. Hash value is a numeric value of fixed length that uniquely identifies data. Miners use their computer to zero in on a hash value less than the target and whoever is the first to crack it would be considered as the one who mined the block and is eligible to get a rewarded.

The reward for mining a block is now 12.5 bitcoins.
Earlier, only cryptography enthusiasts served as miners. However, as cryptocurrencies gained in popularity and increased in value, mining is now considered a lucrative business. Consequently, several people and enterprises have started investing in warehouses and hardware. As enterprises jumped into the fray, unable to compete, bitcoin miners have begun to join open pools, combining resources to effectively compete. Bank of New York Mellon Corp BK 2.3% has been running an internal blockchain platform for U.S. Treasury bond settlements since early 2016, a Marketwatch report quoting Morgan Stanley said. The private nature of the platform has kept it out of the regulatory purview. Once the bank decides to roll it out to clients and use it commercially, regulatory oversight might come into

the picture. A complete mining kit consists of graphics cards, a processor, power supply, memory, cabling and a fan, which would cost between $2,400 and $3,800 on Amazon.com, Inc. AMZN 0.85%, according to Bloomberg. The top three mining hardware, according to 99bitcoins.com, are Avalon6, AntMiner S7 and AntMiner S9. Given that existing GPUs aren't powerful enough, now miners are flocking to application-specific integrated circuits, or ASICs. To circumvent this shortcoming, Nvidia and AMD are said to be working on GPUs, which could be used specifically for the purpose. The two companies who are dominant in consumer-grade mining hardware are Canaan and Bitmain. Bitmain, based in Beijing, does mining as well as manufactures mining hardware.

Mining Pools And Their Share Of Mining

Mining pools are concentrated in China, which boasts of 81 percent of the network hash rate. Why Mining Chips Are A Fickle Revenue Stream For companies such as AMD and Nvidia, which have dominant positions in the gaming chip market, a focus away from their core business may not be a prudent course of action. As seen, these companies may have to bring out new GPUs designed exclusively for this purpose to pose a real threat to the ASIC chips, which are predominantly manufactured by the Chinese, who are notorious for their low-cost market positioning. How viable is the spend on such exclusive chips is a moot point. Additionally, national governments and exchanges are mulling over regulation of the whole realm of cryptocurrencies. Japan has recently introduced legislation to protect users after Tokyo-based Bitcoin exchange Mt Gox collapsed in 2014. Similarly, introducing taxation such as capital gains tax on Bitcoin sales may also impede the cryptocurrency industry.

CHAPTER FOUR
HOW TO MINE BITCOIN

Crypto Currency is electronic money that is not of any particular country and not produced by any government-controlled bank. These digital currencies are also known as Altcoins. They are based on cryptography. This currency is produced by a mathematical process so that it will not lose its value as a result of large circulation. There are different types of Crypto Currency such as Litecoin, Bitcoin, Peercoin and Namecoin. The transactions using the digital currency are carried out using the mechanism of mining. Those who want to do this process, generate the currency in their computers with the help of the software meant for this purpose. Once the currency is created, it is recorded in the network, thereby announcing its existence. The value of Altcoins went up to amazing levels during the last couple of years and as a result, its mining is now a highly profitable business. Many companies started making chips that are exclusively used for running the cryptographic algorithms of this process. Antminer is a popular ASIC hardware used for drawing out Bitcoin. Mining Bitcoins: Antminer comes with different specifications such as U1 and U2+. Both U1 and U2+ are about the same size. While U1 has a default hash rate of 1.6 GH/s, U2+ has the hash rate of 2.0 GH/s. The process of entering the Bitcoins transactions in the public ledger is known as Bitcoin mining. The new They are introduced into the system through this process. The Bitcoin miner can earn transaction fees and subsidy for the newly created coins. ASIC (Application Specific Integrated Circuit) is a microchip specifically designed for this process. When compared to previous technologies, they are faster. The service offered by the Bitcoin miner is based on specifiedperformance. They provide a specific level of production capacity for a set price. Mining Altcoins: Though this process is very easy, they are of much lesser value when compared to Bitcoin. Because of their lower value Altcoins are not as popular as the other. Those who want to earn from their Altcoins may run the appropriate program on their PCs. The Altcoins use the mining algorithm known as 'Scrypt'. They cannot be solved using the ASIC chips. The miners can then either spend the currency or swap them for Bitcoins at the Crypto Currency Exchange. For producting Altcoins, the miner has to write a short script for the command prompt. Those who write the script perfectly are ensured of success. One has to decide whether to join a pool or to produce alone. Joining the pool is the ideal choice for Altcoin miners. When most people think of cryptocurrency they might as well be thinking of cryptic currency. Very few people seem to know what it is and for some reason everyone seems to be talking about it as if they do. This report will hopefully demystify all the aspects of cryptocurrency so that by the time you're finished reading you will have a pretty good idea of what it is and what it's all about. You may find that cryptocurrency is for you or you may not but at least you'll be able to speak with a degree of certainty and knowledge that others won't possess. There are many people who have already reached millionaire status by dealing in cryptocurrency. Clearly there's a lot of money in this brand new industry. Cryptocurrency is electronic currency, short and simple. However, what's not so short and simple is exactly how it comes to have value. Cryptocurrency is a digitized, virtual, decentralized currency produced by the application of cryptography, which, according to Merriam Webster dictionary, is the "computerized encoding and decoding of information". Cryptography is the foundation that makes debit cards, computer banking and eCommerce systems possible. Cryptocurrency isn't backed by banks; it's not backed by a government, but by an extremely complicated arrangement of algorithms. Cryptocurrency is electricity which is encoded into complex strings of algorithms. What lends monetary value is their intricacy and their security from hackers. The way that crypto currency is made is simply too difficult to reproduce. Cryptocurrency is in direct opposition to what is called fiat money. Fiat money is currency that gets its worth from government ruling or law. The dollar, the yen, and the Euro are all examples. Any currency that is defined as legal tender is fiat money.

Unlike fiat money, another part of what makes crypto currency valuable is that, like a commodity such as silver and gold, there's only a finite amount of it. Only 21,000,000 of these extremely complex algorithms were produced. No more, no less. It can't be altered by printing more of it, like a government printing more money to pump up the system without backing. Or by a bank altering a digital ledger, something the Federal Reserve will instruct banks to do to adjust for inflation. Cryptocurrency is a means to purchase, sell, and invest that completely avoids both government oversight and banking systems tracking the movement of your money. In a world economy that is destabilized, this system can become a stable force. Cryptocurrency also gives you a great deal of anonymity. Unfortunately this can lead to misuse by a criminal element using crypto currency to their own ends just as regular money can be misused. However, it can also keep the government from tracking your every purchase and invading your personal privacy. Cryptocurrency comes in quite a few forms. Bitcoin was the first and is the standard from which all other cryptocurrencies pattern themselves. All are produced by meticulous alpha-numerical computations from a complex coding tool. Some other cryptocurrencies are Litecoin, Namecoin, Peercoin, Dogecoin, and Worldcoin, to name a few. These are called altcoins as a generalized name. The prices of each are regulated by the supply of the specific cryptocurrency and the demand that the market has for that currency. The way cryptocurrency is brought into existence is quite fascinating. Unlike gold, which has to be mined from the ground, cryptocurrency is merely an entry in a virtual ledger which is stored in various computers around the world. These entries have to be 'mined' using mathematical algorithms. Individual users or, more likely, a group of users run computational analysis to find particular series of data, called blocks. The 'miners' find data that produces an exact pattern to the cryptographic algorithm. At that point, it's applied to the series, and they've found a block. After an equivalent data series on the block matches up with the algorithm, the block of data has been unencrypted. The miner gets a reward of a specific amount of cryptocurrency. As time goes on, the amount of the reward decreases as the cryptocurrency becomes scarcer. Adding to that, the complexity of the algorithms in the search for new blocks is also increased. Computationally, it becomes harder to find a matching series. Both of these scenarios come together to decrease the speed in which cryptocurrency is created. This imitates the difficulty and scarcity of mining a commodity like gold. Now, anyone can be a miner. The originators of Bitcoin made the mining tool open source, so it's free to anyone. However, the computers they use run 24 hours a day, seven days a week. The algorithms are extremely complex and the CPU is running full tilt. Many users have specialized computers made specifically for mining cryptocurrency. Both the user and the specialized computer are called miners. Miners (the human ones) also keep ledgers of transactions and act as auditors, so that a coin isn't duplicated in any way. This keeps the system from being hacked and from running amok. They're paid for this work by receiving new cryptocurrency every week that they maintain their operation. They keep their cryptocurrency in specialized files on their computers or other personal devices. These files are called wallets. Let's recap by going through a few of the definitions we've learned:

- Cryptocurrency: electronic currency; also called digital currency.
- Fiat money: any legal tender; government backed, used in banking system.
- Bitcoin: the original and gold standard of crypto currency.
- Altcoin: other cryptocurrencies that are patterned from the same processes as Bitcoin, but with slight variations in their coding.
- Miners: an individual or group of individuals who use their own resources (computers, electricity, space) to mine digital coins.

o Also a specialized computer made specifically for finding new coins through computing series of algorithms.
- Wallet: a small file on your computer where you store your digital money.

Conceptualizing the cryptocurrency system in a nutshell:

- Electronic money.
- Mined by individuals who use their own resources to find the coins.
- A stable, finite system of currency. For example, there are only 21,000,000 Bitcoins produced for all time.
- Does not require any government or bank to make it work.
- Pricing is decided by the amount of the coins found and used which is combined with the demand from the public to possess them.
- There are several forms of crypto currency, with Bitcoin being first and foremost.
- Can bring great wealth, but, like any investment, has risks.

Most people find the concept of cryptocurrency to be fascinating. It's a new field that could be the next gold mine for many of them. If you find that cryptocurrency is something you'd like to learn more about then you've found the right report. However, I've barely touched the surface in this report. There is much, much more to cryptocurrency than what I've gone through here.

How To Mine Bitcoin

When Bitcoin was first introduced in 2009, mining the world's first and premier cryptocurrency needed little more than a home PC — and not even a fast one at that. Today, the barrier for entry is far higher if you want to make any kind of profit doing it. That doesn't mean it's impossible, but it's not the homebrew industry it once was. Before we discuss how to mine Bitcoins yourself, it's important to note that although there is uncertainty in everything cryptocurrency related, mining is arguably the most volatile. Hardware price fluctuations, changes in Bitcoin-mining difficulty and even the lack of a guarantee of a payout at the end of all your hard work, make it a riskier investment than even buying Bitcoins directly. Because of this and general market volatility, it can be difficult to know how much profit you will make from mining. 2018 saw the mining market plummet in regards to profit and shoot up when it comes to barriers to entry. Unless there's a significant Bitcoin tech change, this is likely to stay the same. A single Bitcoin is valued at around $9,100, at the time of writing, but mining that can cost not much less. In the end, buying Bitcoin directly at least gives you something for your money immediately. It's certainly worth considering before you go down the mining route.

Step 1: Pick your mining company

Hashflare
Cloud mining is the practice of renting mining hardware (or a portion of their hashing power) and having someone else do the mining for you. You are typically 'paid' for your investment with Bitcoin. Even if the hardware isn't used for mining Bitcoin. As with general investing, it's important to do your research, because there are a lot of companies out there which purport to be the best and even the largest have their detractors. A number of cloud mining companies have come and gone over the years, including ones we've spoken to and validated directly, like HashFlare, which told Digital Trends in an interview that every one of its customers has turned a profit using its service. In late-2019, you're far better off going with a company like Bitcoin Pool, which is the cloud mining arm of Bitcoin.com, an established and respected cloud mining entity. It's expensive to get started, but one of the best options out there. For a broader range of options, CryptoCompare maintains a list of mining companies with user reviews and ratings, though be aware there are a lot of reviewers looking to shill their referral codes in the comment section.

Step 2: Choose a mining package

Bitcoin Pool
Once you have picked a cloud mining provider and signed up, you need to pick a mining package. That will typically involve choosing a certain amount of hashing power and cross-referencing that with how much you can afford to pay. Typically, paying more will give you a better return or you will turn a profit quicker, but that's not always the case. Most cloud mining companies will help you decide by giving you a calculation based on the current market value of Bitcoin, the difficulty of Bitcoin mining, and cross-refer-

encing that with the hashing power you're renting. However, it's important to note that those numbers can and do change, so it is important to look at market trends and estimate where Bitcoin may be going before choosing your contract. What may be profitable now, may not be if Bitcoin's value crashes. As much as companies like Bitcoin Pool offer their own calculators too, we'd suggest using a third-party alternative just to alleviate the potential for any bias that might sneak in to the calculation. Some cloud mining companies will sell you a contract on a "pre-sale" basis. That is effectively asking you to pay upfront for a contract that won't begin for weeks or months when new hardware becomes available. In most circumstances that is not advisable because there is no way to guarantee those contracts will be profitable when they start and not even a concrete indication of when that will happen.

Step 3: Pick a mining pool
After choosing your contract, most cloud mining companies will ask you to pick a mining pool. That's where you choose a global mining team to join. It's a method of increasing the chance of earning Bitcoin through mining and it's a standard practice in the cloud and personal mining. There are pros and cons of different pools that go beyond the scope of this article, but joining an established and proven pool with low fees is likely to be your best bet. One of the most popular and dependable pools for new miners is Slush Pool, but you should always do your own research. Like companies, many pools aren't trustworthy.

Step 4: Select a wallet
Once you've completed that step your cloud mining can begin and within a few days or weeks, you should start to see your cloud mining account begin to fill with Bitcoin. Withdrawing it and putting it into a secure wallet of your own is a good plan as soon as you have a small holding, though

some cloud miners will allow you to reinvest your earnings for greater hashing power. Whatever you do though, you need to decide what you're going to do with your bitcoins in the long term. While there are many products and services you can purchase with bitcoins, prices can fluctuate, and you may have to do even more research to see if you're getting a good deal. We can also help you trade your bitcoin for a different cryptocurrency or sell it directly for cash.

"Hodling," that is, holding your Bitcoin for the future, is also a viable strategy. Many people believe that its value will go up in time. While we aren't financial advisors and wouldn't suggest you do anything in particular with your Bitcoin, if you do plan to hold it, you want to consider a secure, potentially even hardware, wallet to store it in.

What if I want to mine with my own hardware?
Due to the high costs involved, mining Bitcoin yourself is only recommendable if you have ready access to plentiful and more importantly, cheap electricity and a powerful network connection. Before investing in any hardware or mining setups, it is imperative you use a Bitcoin mining calculator to see if you can actually turn a profit with all costs considered. If you can, you'll need to pick the right ASIC miner to do it with. The best method is to consult mining machine profitability to see which miners are currently turning a profit. The site Asicminervalue.com is particularly helpful here, showing a constantly updated list of miners and how profitable they are. Note that the most profitable machines make between $10 and $30 profit per day, and costs thousands of dollars to set up. Recouping your costs are far from guaranteed, so proceed cautiously.

Bitcoin mining is far removed from the average Bitcoin owner these days, but that doesn't change how important it is. It's the process that helps the cryptocurrency function as intended and what continues to introduce new Bitcoins to digital wallets all over the world. Collecting cryptocurrency can be boiled down to a simple premise: "Miners," as they are known, purchase powerful computing chips designed for the process and use them to run specifically crafted software day and night. That software forces the system to complete complicated calculations — imagine them digging through layers of digital rock. If all goes to plan, the miners are rewarded with some Bitcoin at the end of their toils.

Why do we need mining?

Bitcoin works differently from traditional currencies. Where dollars, pounds, and euros, for instance, are handled by banks and financial institutions that collectively confirm when transactions occur, Bitcoin operates on the basis of a public ledger system. In order for transactions to be confirmed — to avoid the same Bitcoin from being spent twice, for example — a number of Bitcoin nodes, operated by miners around the world, need to give it their seal of approval. For that, they are rewarded the transaction fees paid by those conducting them, and while there are still new Bitcoins to be made — there are currently more than 18.3 million of a maximum 21 million — a separate reward too, in order to incentivize the practice. In taking part in mining, miners create new Bitcoins to add to the general circulation, while facilitating the very transactions that make Bitcoin a functional cryptocurrency. Mining is a risky process though. It not only takes heavy lifting from the mining chips themselves, but boatloads of electricity, powerful cooling, and a strong network connection. The reward at the end isn't even guaranteed either, so it should never be entered into lightly.

How it works

The reason it's called mining isn't that it involves a physical act of digging. Bitcoin are entirely digital tokens that don't require explosive excavation or panning streams, but they do have their own form of prospecting and recovery, which is where the "mining" nomenclature comes from. Prospective miners download and run bespoke mining software — of which there are several popular options — and often join a pool of other miners doing the same thing. Together or alone, the software compiles recent Bitcoin transactions into blocks and proves their validity by calculating a "proof of work," which covers all of the data in those blocks. That involves the mining hardware taking a huge number of guesses at a particular integer over and over until they find the correct one. It's a computationally intense process that is further hampered by deliberate increases in difficulty as more and more miners attempt to create the next block in the chain. That's why people join pools and why only the most powerful of application specific integrated circuit (ASIC) mining hardware is effective at mining Bitcoins today. The individual miner or pool that is the first to create the proof of work for a block is rewarded with transaction fees for those confirmed transactions and a subsidy of Bitcoin. That subsidy is made up of new Bitcoin, which are generated through the process of mining. That will continue to happen until all 21 million have been mined. There is no guarantee that any one miner or mining pool will generate the correct integer needed to confirm a block and thereby earn the reward. That's precisely why miners join pools. Although their reward is far smaller should they mine the next block since it's shared among all members of the pool, the chances of earning such a reward are far greater as a collective and a return on any investment much more likely.

The future of mining

What is Bitcoin Mining - ASIC miner
Bitcoin was originally designed to allow anyone to take part in the mining process with a home computer and thereby enjoy the process of mining themselves, receiving a reward on occasion for their service. ASIC miners have made that impossible for anyone unable to invest thousands of dollars and use cheap and plentiful electricity. That's why cloud mining has become so popular, recently entering the news cycle as a Nintendo Switch title, Cooking Mama: Cookstar, was rumored to include secret cryptocurrency mining software written into the code. Although hardware has pushed many miners out of the practice though, there are safeguards in place that prevent all remaining Bitcoins from being mined in a short period of time. The first of those is a (likely) ever-increasing difficulty in the mining calculations that must be made. Every 2,016 blocks — at a rate of six blocks an hour, roughly every two weeks — the mining difficulty is recalculated. Mostly it increases as more miners and mining hardware join the network, but if the overall mining power were to reduce, then the difficulty would decrease to maintain a roughly 10-minute block-generation time. The purpose of that relatively hard 10-minute time is because that way the number of Bitcoins being generated by the process will be slow and steady, and thereby mostly controlled. This is compounded by the reduction in reward for blocks mined every 210,000 blocks. Each time that threshold is reached, the reward is halved. In early 2020, mining a block rewards 12.5 Bitcoins, which is worth around $80,000. In the future, as mining rewards decrease, the transaction rewarded to miners will make up a larger percentage of miner income. At the rate with which Bitcoin mining difficulty is increasing, mining hardware development is progressing, and rewards are decreasing, projections for the final Bitcoins being mined edge into the

22nd century. What is Bitcoin halving and when does it happen?

Bitcoin is scheduled to have its third halving event this May, and if history repeats itself, an increase in Bitcoin is sure to follow. As the most popular form of cryptocurrency (and the blockchain technology that powers it) Bitcoin is now widely accepted around the world and has a growing number of applications. Since there is nothing backing Bitcoin other than what people are willing to pay for it, the cryptocurrency can experience such huge swings in its value, and one of those ways is through halving. If you're new to Bitcoin or unfamiliar with the term, we've broken down what to expect next month during the third Bitcoin halving.

What is Bitcoin halving?

Bitcoin halving is essentially when the number of Bitcoins rewarded for processing transactions is cut in half, which maintains the fixed supply of Bitcoin. Bitcoin halving is a reduction in the amount of Bitcoins rewarded to miners for completing a set of Bitcoin transactions, known as a block. Bitcoin halving events happen approximately every 210,000 blocks.

When is Bitcoin halving happening?

Bitcoin halving has so far happened every four years since the cryptocurrency came about in 2009. Halving has taken place twice, the first being in November 2012, according to Forbes. That halving saw an increase from $11 to $1,000, although the growth didn't occur until a year later. A second Bitcoin halving happened again in July 2016, which saw Bitcoin increase a year later from $700 to $20,000. These two halvings suggest that when the future supply of Bitcoin declines during a halving, the demand for Bitcoin will usually stay the same, which pushes the price up. Based on this, we could observe similar price increases from past halvings in the upcoming one.

What to expect from Bitcoin halving
Tim Draper, an entrepreneur who has made billions from Bitcoin, told BlockTV in a December interview that next month's Bitcoin halving could result cause the price of a Bitcoin to jump to $250,000, which would be the most significant halving increase in Bitcoin's history. Draper added the increase could happen in a time frame from six months to a year after the halving.

Should you buy during a halving?
Those that are interested in Bitcoin should consider buying right now before the next halving event. Theoretically, you should purchase new Bitcoin now since the number of new Bitcoins put in circulation every day will be cut in half as the halving approaches.

CHAPTER FIVE
BITCOIN MINING METHODS

Bitcoin mining is the method in which transactions on the Bitcoin blockchain are confirmed and processed. If there were no Bitcoin miners, the Bitcoin cryptocurrency would cease to function as no transactions would be confirmed.

Those who perform the mining process are referred to as Bitcoin miners and they're rewarded for their work with a percentage of the transaction fee charged to the Bitcoin user. Mining Bitcoin can be an effective way to earn extra money and many individuals have now become full-time Bitcoin miners, though there are risks to crypto mining. Here are the three main ways to mine Bitcoin and start earning money.

Beginner: Using a Bitcoin Mining App

The easiest way to start mining Bitcoin is to simply download an app that does everything for you. Bitcoin Miner is a Windows 10 app that's free to download and use on Windows 10 PCs and mobile devices.

Once the Bitcoin Miner app is downloaded, users simply need to enter their Bitcoin wallet's address in the Payout Address settings screen and then press the prominent Start button. That's all there is to it.

The more powerful your device is, the more Bitcoin transactions it will be able to process. This means that a Windows Phone may not earn much Bitcoin but a Windows 10 computer that can perform heavy duty tasks like video editing and playing major video game titles does have the potential to earn the equivalent of several hundred dollars a day.

Beginner: Mine Bitcoin in the Cloud

A popular but controversial way to get in on the cryptocurrency mining craze is to pay someone else to do it for you. Referred to as cloud mining, this process involves signing up for an account on a third-party's website and paying them to mine Bitcoin and other cryptocurrencies for you. Typically, the more money you pay, the more cryptocurrency your account will be able to mine. However, the slim margins and volatility of cryptocurrencies cast doubt on your ability to make a profit. Cloud mining contracts usually last for a minimum of a year, though some can continue indefinitely. Mined cryptocurrency is sent to your designated wallet address on a regular basis, which makes it a way to earn residual income on a weekly (or sometimes daily) basis. The cryptocurrency that's mined sometimes covers the cost of the initial payment, but there's no guarantee. Services like Genesis Mining offer Bitcoin mining contracts in addition to Litecoin, Ethereum, Monero, and a range of other cryptocurrencies. Just be sure to do your own research before investing in any of them.

Advanced: Building a Bitcoin Mining Rig

Those looking to really invest in cryptocurrency mining will need to buy an application-specific integrated circuits (ASIC) hardware device, often referred to as a mining rig. These are essentially processors that are made solely for mining Bitcoin and other cryptocoins, and they're intended to run non-stop all day, every day.
ASIC miners are generally quite expensive and sell for several thousand dollars. Running such a device also consumes a lot of electricity so it can take a while, often over a year of continuous mining, to begin earning a profit.

The most-popular brand of ASIC miners is Bitmain with its line of Antminer miners. They often release newer models that are more efficient at mining Bitcoin, use less energy, and provide consumers with comprehensive support for both advanced and novice miners. When using an ASIC mining rig, you'll need to download advanced mining software and join a mining pool. The software will tell the ASIC what to mine, where to mine, and who to send the mined Bitcoin to, while the mining pool is a group of other miners that choose to help each other mine together and share the rewards between them. The most commonly recommended mining pool and program is Slush Pool and CGminer, respectively. However, those using a Bitmain miner may prefer to use their own program and mining pool due to the convenience and user-friendly interface.

Bitcoin Mining Pros and Cons

What We Like
• Earn extra money.
• Supports preferred cryptocurrency.
What We Don't Like
• Consumes money, time, and energy.
• No guarantee of profits.

In addition to earning extra money, mining a cryptocurrency can also be a way to support your preferred coin. Miners are needed to process all transactions on a crypto coin's blockchain so the more miners there are, the faster and more stable the coin will be.
Mining Bitcoin and other cryptocurrencies consumes a lot of money, time, and resources. For most people it can be almost as rewarding to simply purchase some Bitcoin from a service like Coinbase or CoinJar and let it increase in value while sitting in a wallet doing nothing.

Coin Mining: What Is an 'Accepted Share'?

Once you're ready to start mining for cryptocoins, you'll start learning about shares. Accepted Shares and rejected shares represent scorekeeping in your mining software. Shares describe how much work your computer is contributing to the mining group.

Why Do Accepted Shares Matter?
Accepted shares and rejected shares. More accepted shares are good; it means your work is counting substantially towards discovering new cryptocoins. The more accepted shares you contribute, the more pool payout for each coin block that is found. Ideally, you want 100 percent of your shares accepted because that means that every single computation on your computer is counted towards a coin discovery.

What Are Rejected Shares?
Rejected shares represent work that will not be applied toward a blockchain discovery, and they will therefore not be paid for. Rejected shares typically occur when your computer was busy grinding a cryptocoin share problem and it did not submit the results in time to be counted towards a coin discovery. Rejected share work is discarded. Rejected shares are inevitable, especially in any mining pool with more than a dozen users. It's just a fact of cryptocoin mining. Very serious coin miners tweak their graphics processing unit to maximize how often their computer submits work every second.

How Cryptocoin Mining Works

Most cryptocoin mining is all about solving mathematical problems, which in turn act as raffle tickets. Each problem solved is called a proof of work result and counts as one raffle ticket. Every time a predetermined quantity of proof-of-work results is generated, the system draws a raffle number, and one proof-of-work result is awarded a block of new cryptocoins. Every miner who contributed to solving that particular block will get some kind of proportionate share of the rewards. Without accepted shares, then, a miner gets nothing. It's All About Contributing Your Computer Power to the Mining Group

Because proof-of-work problems are difficult to solve, results are best achieved when users combine their computers into a pool, with each person's computer contributing a share of the effort. As your personal machine achieves its proof-of-work results, it submits its results to the group. The faster you can solve proof-of-work problems, the more results you can submit to the group every minute. If your machine submits its results before the new coin block is found, that's an accepted share. When the group of people is rewarded with newly minted coins, it distributes those earnings across people proportionately by their accepted shares.

Bitcoin Mining Pools: How To Find and Join One

Finding a mining pool is a valuable part of mining Bitcoin and other cryptocurrencies. Mining pools allow Bitcoin miners to combine their efforts and share the rewards earned. Using a mining pool almost always results in higher earnings than mining alone and there are numerous pools to choose from, some officially managed by companies and others run by dedicated users.Bitcoin mining is the process in which transactions are confirmed on the Bitcoin blockchain. People who partake in mining are referred to as Bitcoin miners. Bitcoin miners use dedicated software on their computers to process transactions. The more powerful a miner's computer is, the more transactions they can process and the more Bitcoin they earn as a reward for their efforts. Mining rewards consist of the small fees charged to the person who initiated the Bitcoin transaction (for example, a person buying a coffee with a Bitcoin smartphone wallet). Occasionally the Bitcoin blockchain will release new Bitcoin during the mining process and this largess is divided up among the members of the Bitcoin mining pool that unlocked it.

What is a Mining Pool?

Joining a Bitcoin mining pool is kind of like buying lottery tickets with a group of friends and agreeing to split the prize money among yourselves if one of you wins. You have a greater chance of winning a little bit of money more often this way than simply buying one ticket by yourself and hoping to get the grand prize once. Each Bitcoin mining pool offers a numerical address inputted into the custom settings in the Bitcoin mining software. Most mining apps and services support their own official mining pools although many online communities have also created their own. Some pools can be more profitable (i.e. earn more rewards) than others so it can be worth experimenting with different pools on a weekly or monthly basis. Using a custom pool isn't a requirement, though, and is usually something done by advanced miners. Other mineable cryptocurrencies also have their own mining pools.

Using a Default Mining Pool
Most Bitcoin mining apps and services run their own official pools. These official mining pools are typically the de-

fault option but they can be changed to a custom pool in the application settings.

Official Bitcoin mining pools are usually a reliable option for most people as they often have a lot of other Bitcoin miners already mining in them and also receive technical support and upgrades by the company behind the app or service it's related to. Examples of services that provide a default mining pool are the Windows 10 Bitcoin Miner app and the popular Bitcoin mining rig hardware manufacturer, Bitmain. Should You Change Mining Pools?

Change Bitcoin mining pools to experiment and see if a different pool will increase your earnings. In most cases, using a default, official mining pool should be perfectly fine, however.

One good reason to change mining pools can be if you wish to mine a different cryptocurrency. The Windows 10 Bitcoin Miner app can also mine Litecoin, for example, by simply entering the address of a Litecoin mining pool in the Custom Miner option in Settings.

If the type of cryptocurrency mining pool is changed, the payout wallet address should also be changed. For example, if you're mining from a Litecoin mining pool, make sure that your payout wallet address is for a Litecoin wallet. Using an incorrect cryptocurrency wallet will result in an error and you will lose your earnings. There can be some exceptions to this rule where a mining pool could allow you to mine one cryptocoin such as Ethereum and be paid in Bitcoin. The pool's official website or discussion forums will mention if this duality is possible.

How to Find Another Mining Pool

The most-popular alternative Bitcoin mining pools are Slush Pool and CGminer. Slush Pool was the first Bitcoin mining pool ever created and, while it is no longer the biggest, it has a solid community built up around it and a lot of support material available to help new miners get started.

The most convenient place to find alternative Bitcoin mining pools is Crypto Compare. The site lists almost all available pools and lets you sort them by specific details and rank them out of five stars for quality and reliability.

Here are three things to look out for when searching for a mining pool.
• Fee: The fee percentage is what the owner of the pool will take from your own overall earnings. This can range from 0 percent to 10 percent. While joining a pool without a fee sounds tempting, pools usually have low or no fees because they have no users and are trying to attract new members. It can often be worth joining a better-quality pool with a lot of users and paying a higher fee as that could earn you more in the long run.
• Country of Origin: While you can join a pool located anywhere around the world, joining one closer to where you are will result in a better experience and higher earnings.
• Reputation: The cryptocurrency space can be quite political with some mining pools actively trying to sabotage the evolving Bitcoin technology by deliberately mining Bitcoin in a way that slows down transactions on the blockchain or refusing to switch to a more advanced version of Bitcoin that could be more secure and cheaper for users. A Twitter search of a mining pool's name will usually reveal any negative aspects relating to a mining pool and its miners. Some pools to avoid are BTC Nuggets, F2Pool, and AntPool.

Mining Pools Don't Replace Hardware

A pool, no matter how great of a reputation it has, cannot make up for a lack of quality mining hardware. Mining pool earnings are still calculated on how much your own computer can mine so you will still need to invest in building a mining rig if you hope to make anything worthwhile.

If purchasing a mining rig isn't an option for you, cloud mining could be a viable alternative because of its cheaper price and ease of use.

How You Could Lose Out While Mining Cryptocoins

There is a lot at risk when you mine for cryptocoins. Rewards can certainly be big in the long-run, but it's a good idea to think of cryptocurrency mining as investing in the stock market before 1929, when the government did not insure banks and investors lost millions of dollars. Cryptocoin is regulated by any government; that's the point of digital currency. Here's what to know before you mine for coins.

The 5 Biggest Risks of Cryptocurrency Mining
There are some substantial risks to be aware of when mining any cryptocurrency:
1. Losing your digital wallet of coins: You can lose your wallet either by forgetting your password, which locks you out or by physically losing the wallet when your hard drive breaks or your online wallet provider goes out of business.
2. Dishonest mining pool organizers: If you join a mining pool that is run by dishonest administrators, they could skim coins from your earnings or take your earnings altogether and close shop.
3. Electricity costs could make your mining unprofitable: For most mining computers, a cost of 14 cents/kilowatt hour is the most you want to pay for your mining hobby. Above 14 cents, mining currencies such as Bitcoin, Litecoin, Peercoin, and Feathercoin are not worth the investment. Similarly, if you invest more than a several hundred dollars in mining hardware, at a rate of two dollars profit per day (and assuming there is no leap in coin value),

it could take two years for you to pay off your hardware investment.
4. Black Hat Hackers: It is possible that a talented hacker can break into your mining pool and empty the users' wallets, including yours.
5. The cryptocurrency you choose could drop in value instead of grow. Just like gold or any other commodity, there is a chance that the market value of your cryptocoins will fall, and you will be sitting on top of a pile of pennies instead of a pile of dollars.

How Do I Reduce These Coin Mining Risks?

While no moneymaking venture is ever risk-free, you can certainly reduce your cryptocoin mining risks. Here are a few suggestions for managing your coin mining vulnerabilities:

• The best prevention against being hacked is a combination of hardware and personal habit. Put your coin wallet database on a detachable hard drive or a USB stick that you detach from your computer and network when you're not using it. Then, transfer your coins from your online storage into your detachable wallet so they do not accumulate online.
• Follow a personal habit of backing up your wallet every two days, keep your password written down in a safe place, and keep a personal wallet on your home computer to lower the risk of losing your wallet.
• Find a reputable mining pool where the members are active in a forum and keep each other honest by keeping constant eyes on the pool operations.
• Some electricity providers allow you to lock in your per-kilowatt-hour fee for a year or two. If you can do so at 14 cents or less per kilowatt hour, then do it. 10 cents per kwh

and less is excellent, not just for mining but for your own benefit as a consumer.

What Are Smart Contracts and Cryptocoin Accounts?
What is a smart contract? Does it have anything to do with cryptocoin accounts or cryptocoin wallets? There's a lot to learn about cryptocurrency; here's a good look at these three topics and how they intersect. Cryptocoins, or cryptocurrencies, are a new form of digital currency powered by a type of technology called a blockchain. Bitcoin is one example of a cryptocurrency. Ethereum, Ripple, Litecoin, and Monero are some others that are commonly used. This new technology has seen the arrival of a host of new words and phrases that many wouldn't have even heard of a decade ago and they can cause some confusing amongst new consumers looking to get into the exciting world of cryptocurrency.

Two of these new crypto phrases cause the most confusion are cryptocoin accounts and smart contracts. Here's what you need to know.

Cryptocoin Accounts Don't Really Exist

Because cryptocurrency is usually talked about as a new technology, it's understandable for those who are new to it to think that they have to sign up for a cryptocoin account in the same way that people need to sign up for Facebook and Twitter before they can begin using those services.

In reality though, all cryptocoins are simply a form of currency and don't have a direct account system tied to them. You don't need to create a dollar account to send and receive dollars. You don't need a Bitcoin account to use Bitcoin either.

When casual crypto users mention a cryptocoin account they could be referencing (incorrectly) a cryptocurrency wallet or a third-party service which manages Bitcoin and other cryptocoins.

What's a Cryptocurrency Wallet?

A wallet is a piece of software that contains the private keys that grant access to cryptocurrency funds on their respective blockchains. Without a wallet, you cannot access a cryptocurrency. Most of the crypto smartphone apps you see in the iTunes or Google Play stores are software wallets for holding, receiving, and spending cryptocurrency. You can also download software wallets onto your computer such as the Exodus Wallet. Actual physical devices that are used to store and use cryptocoins are called hardware wallets and these have software wallets on them but use the physical keys as an extra layer of security.

What Are Popular Cryptocoin Account Services?

Popular services such as Coinbase and CoinJar sort of work as cryptocurrency banks. They allow users to create (service not cryptocoin) accounts on their websites which can be used to buy, trade, and send Bitcoin, Litecoin, Ethereum, and other cryptocurrencies.

It's important to remember that these are third-party services that can be used to help people use cryptocurrency. Cryptocoins are similar to regular money in that there are many ways to get them and some are more trustworthy than others.

What is a Smart Contract?

A smart contract is simply a protocol that's used to automatically verify, process, or negotiate a specific set of conditions during a transaction on a blockchain. They're sort of like contracts that are agreed upon by both parties and are able to be verified by the blockchain itself without the involvement of any third-parties or the authorities.

Because of the nature of blockchain technology, the processing of information via a smart contract should, in theory, be faster and more secure than the traditional method of sending files online or physically relaying data in person. There is less chance of mistakes being made as data is processed instantaneously and the blockchain itself can check immediately for accuracy. Not all cryptocurrencies support smart contracts however. Bitcoin, which is easily the most-famous cryptocurrency, doesn't use smart contracts at all while many others like Ethereum do. In fact, smart contracts are one of the reason that Ethereum has garnered so much attention among programmers and developers. Smart contracts are a technology that can be added to cryptocoins by the currency's developers though so while a coin may not have the capability to perform a smart contract today, it could in the future. Potential use cases for smart contracts include managing auctions and investments, scheduling payments, managing data, and crowdfunding.

Are Smart Contracts Important?

Smart contracts could be important for the numerous ways they could improve a variety of industries but for casual cryptocurrency users who simply want to use their cryptocoins to go shopping or keep as an investment, it's not really something they should worry too much about. It really depends on who you are and how you use your crypto.

What Is Bitcoin Cash and How Does It Work?

Bitcoin Cash is a popular cryptocurrency that was spun off from the original Bitcoin blockchain as part of a fork in 2017. Fans of Bitcoin Cash often praise its potential for processing more transactions at a faster rate than Bitcoin and it's widely supported by most cryptocurrency wallets, Bitcoin ATMS, and crypto exchanges. A cryptocurrency fork is when a blockchain is copied and given to another group of developers. The copy then becomes a new cryptocurrency that can be re-branded and changed while the original remains intact. Litecoin was created by forking the Bitcoin blockchain, as were Bitcoin Cash and Bitcoin Gold. Bitcoin Cash is also referred to as Bcash in many places and, rather controversially, has also been known to be referred to simply as Bitcoin, which can cause a lot of confusion among casual crypto traders and investors.

BCH vs BTC

The BCH designation is used to identify Bitcoin Cash on trading platforms and in wallets. This is the officially recognized code for the Bitcoin Cash digital currency.

Coinbase
In the early days of Bitcoin Cash, some people used BTH and BCC to refer to Bitcoin Cash. Both have since been phased out and should no longer be used as BTH is now the official designation for Bithereum while BCC is used for the now defunct BitConnect Coin. It's important to remember when trading that only trades using BCH contain Bitcoin Cash. Some may casually refer to Bitcoin Cash as BTC Cash. This is because BTC is the designation for Bitcoin on trading platforms and can be read as Bitcoin.

Bitcoin vs Bitcoin Cash

The Bitcoin Cash vs Bitcoin rivalry has been a constant since the infamous fork in 2017 due to the developers behind each cryptocoin, and their supporters, feeling so passionately about each cryptocurrency. Despite having Bitcoin in its name, Bitcoin Cash is a completely separate cryptocoin than Bitcoin and has its own value and type of wallet addresses. The main argument for Bitcoin Cash over Bitcoin is its support for larger data block sizes which allow it, on paper, to process more transactions on the Bitcoin Cash blockchain. It should be mentioned, though, that projects such as the Lightning Network, a layer of programming that works on top of the Bitcoin blockchain, have increased Bitcoin transaction speeds to the point where speed isn't really an issue anymore. The green Bitcoin Cash logo on the left and the orange Bitcoin logo on the right. Bitcoin, in general, will be supported by most online and offline business that accepts cryptocurrency payments while support for Bitcoin Cash is often less prevalent. Both have solid support from software and hardware cryptocurrency wallets, centralized and decentralized cryptocurrency exchanges, and online marketplaces such as Coinbase. It's unrealistic to expect Bitcoin Cash to overtake Bitcoin in value and usage, however, some may use it as an altcoin. Altcoin is a phrase used by cryptocurrency enthusiasts to refer to any cryptocoin other than Bitcoin. Ethereum, Monero, Litecoin, and all of the other Cryptocurrencies are altcoins.

What Can I Use Bitcoin Cash For?

Bitcoin Cash can be used to make purchases from any businesses that accept the cryptocurrency. A variety of offline businesses and online storefronts accept Bitcoin Cash payments but it's important to check before making a purchase as support for cryptocoins in general has yet to go mainstream and isn't accepted everywhere. There is a difference between Bitcoin and Bitcoin Cash. You cannot send Bitcoin Cash to a Bitcoin address. If you do so, your Bitcoin Cash coins will be lost. You must send Bitcoin Cash transactions to a Bitcoin Cash address and Bitcoin to a Bitcoin address.

What's a Good Bitcoin Cash Wallet?
All of the major cryptocurrency wallets support Bitcoin Cash. Some of the best software wallets for Bitcoin Cash are Exodus and Coinbase Wallet while hardware wallets made by Ledger and Trezor are known for their reliability and safety.

Where Can I Buy Bitcoin Cash?
You can trade other cryptocurrency, such as Bitcoin or Ripple, for Bitcoin Cash on an exchange but the easiest way to get Bitcoin Cash is to perform a swap on ShapeShift or buy some on Coinbase or CoinJar.

Where Can I Sell Bitcoin Cash?
The best way to convert your Bitcoin Cash into real-world fiat money is to use an online service such as CoinJar or Coinbase which can make the trade for you and deposit the money into your bank account. You can also use an ATM that supports Bitcoin Cash deposits and withdrawals but these can be hard to come by.

How Can I Accept Bitcoin Cash Payments?
To receive a payment in Bitcoin Cash from other people, you'll need to set up a Bitcoin Cash wallet either online or within an app. You can also us a physical hardware wallet such as the Ledger S or Ledger X. If you've bought Bitcoin Cash on Coinbase, you'll already have a wallet and can receive payments directly into your Coinbase account. Once you have a Bitcoin Cash wallet, simply share the wallet ad-

dress with the person you want to receive Bitcoin Cash from.

Coinbase
If you run a business, you may want to print out the wallet address' QR code and place it near your register or checkout for customers to scan.

If you plan on getting payments in Bitcoin Cash for work, make sure to check your wallet's balance on your phone, tablet, or computer to ensure that your customer or client has sent you the correct amount.

What is Bitcoin SV?
Similar to how Bitcoin Cash was a fork of Bitcoin, Bitcoin SV is a fork of Bitcoin Cash. The fork was initiated in late-2018 with the aim of creating a cryptocurrency that used the same technology behind the Bitcoin blockchain but would have a larger block size limit than Bitcoin Cash.

The SV in Bitcoin SV stands for Satoshi's Vision. Satoshi was the original creator of Bitcoin whose name true identity remains a mystery. While based on the same technology and containing the word Bitcoin in its name, Bitcoin SV is a completely separate cryptocurrency than Bitcoin Cash and should not be confused with it. Alternative Cryptocurrencies to Bitcoin Cash

Bitcoin Cash may have its fans but the original Bitcoin is consistently more valuable and more popular than it and every other cryptocurrency on the market.

If looking for a non-Bitcoin cryptocoin to invest in or experiment with, Litecoin and Ethereum have both proven themselves to be reliable cryptocurrencies in their own right and have each been around for a relatively long time. Despite its popularity, cryptocurrency is still in its early stages and should be approached with caution when investing. The relatively new cryptocurrency, Tron, is an interesting coin to check out for those with a passion for digital media while Ripple, also relatively new compared to Bitcoin, is growing in popularity and actually set a new daily transaction record in late-2019, sending more money over its blockchain than Bitcoin, Ethereum, Bitcoin Cash, and Litecoin. The aim of the information on this page is to educate the reader on the basics of cryptocurrency investing but it is not intended as financial advice or an endorsement for any specific cryptocurrency. Everyone is solely responsible for their own financial decision and a professional financial adviser should be consulted before making any major money decisions.

CHAPTER SIX
IS BITCOIN A STORE OF VALUE?

A store of value is an asset that's capable of retaining value over time. If you purchased a good store of value today, you could be reasonably certain that its value would not depreciate over time. In the future, you would expect the asset to be worth just as much (if not more so). When you think of such a "safe haven" asset, gold or silver probably come to mind. There are a handful of reasons why these have traditionally held value, which we'll get into shortly.

What makes a good store of value?

To understand what makes a good store of value, let's first explore what might make a poor store of value. If we want something to be preserved for long periods of time, it stands to reason that it needs to be durable.

Consider food. Apples and bananas have some intrinsic value, as humans require nutrition to live. When food is scarce, these items would no doubt be highly valuable. But that doesn't make them a good store of value. They'll be worth a lot less if you keep them in a safe for several years because they'll obviously degrade.

But what about something intrinsically valuable that's also durable? Say, dry pasta? That's better in the long run, but there's still no guarantee that it holds value. Pasta is cheaply produced from readily-available resources. Anyone can flood the market with more pasta, so the pasta in circulation will depreciate in value as supply outweighs demand. Therefore, for something to maintain value, it must also be scarce.

Some consider fiat currencies (dollars, euros, yen) a good way to store wealth as they retain value in the long term. But they're actually poor stores of value because the purchasing power drops significantly as more units are created (just like the pasta). You could withdraw your life savings and stash them under your mattress for twenty years, but they won't have the same purchasing power when you eventually decide to spend them. In the year 2000, $100,000 could buy you a lot more than it can today. This is mainly due to inflation, which refers to the increase in the price of goods and services. In many cases, inflation is caused by an excessive supply of fiat currency due to the government practice of printing more money. To illustrate, suppose that you hold 25% of the total supply of $100 billion – so, $25 billion. Time goes on, and the government decides to print, for instance, an additional $800 billion to stimulate the economy. Your piece of the pie has suddenly dropped to ~3%. There's a lot more money in circulation, so it stands to reason that your share doesn't hold as much purchasing power as it used to.

The loss of purchasing power over time.

The loss of purchasing power over time.

Like our pasta mentioned earlier, dollars are not expensive to produce. The above can happen in a matter of days. With a good store of value, it should be challenging to flood the market with new units. In other words, your piece of the pie should dilute very slowly, if at all. Taking gold as an example, we know that its supply is finite. We also know that it's very difficult to mine. So even if the demand for gold suddenly rises, it's not a matter of firing up a printer to create more. It has to be extracted from the ground, as always. Though there's an influx in demand, supply can't be materially increased to cater to it.

The case for Bitcoin as a store of value

From the early days of Bitcoin, proponents have made the case for the cryptocurrency being more akin to "digital gold" than simple digital currency. In recent years, this narrative has been echoed by many Bitcoin enthusiasts. The store of value thesis for Bitcoin argues that it's one of the soundest assets known to man. Proponents of the thesis believe that Bitcoin is the best way to store wealth such that it isn't devalued over time. Bitcoin is known for wild volatility. It might seem unintuitive that an asset that can lose 20% of its value in a day is considered by many as a store of value. But even factoring in its many drops, it remains the best performing asset class to date.

So, why has Bitcoin been hailed as a store of value?

Scarcity
Perhaps one of the most persuasive arguments for the store of value thesis is that Bitcoin has a finite supply. As you may remember from our article What is Bitcoin?, there will never be more than 21 million bitcoins. The protocol makes sure of this with a hardcoded rule. The only way that new coins can be created is through the process of mining, which is somewhat analogous to how gold is mined. But instead of drilling into the Earth, Bitcoin miners must crack a cryptographic puzzle using computational power. Doing so will earn them fresh coins. As time goes on, the reward diminishes due to events known as halvings. If you guessed that this halves the reward, you'd be absolutely right. In the early days of Bitcoin, the system rewarded 50 BTC to any miner that produced a valid block. During the first halving, this number was reduced to 25 BTC. The subsequent halving cut it in half to 12.5 BTC, and the next one will slash miners' reward to 6.25 bitcoins per block. This process will continue on for another 100+ years until the final fraction

of a coin has entered into circulation. Let's model this similarly to our fiat currency example from earlier. Suppose you bought 25% of the Bitcoin supply (i.e., 5,250,000 coins) many years ago. When you acquired these coins, you knew that your percentage would remain the same because there's no entity capable of adding more coins to the system. There's no government here – well, not in the traditional sense (more on this shortly). So if you bought (and HODLed) 25% of the maximum supply in 2010, you still own 25% of it today.

Decentralization
It's open-source software, you might be thinking. I can copy the code and make my own version with an additional 100 million coins. You could indeed do that. Let's say you clone the software, make the changes, and run a node. Everything seems to be working fine. There's just one problem: there are no other nodes to connect to. You see, as soon as you changed the parameters of your software, members on the Bitcoin network started ignoring you. You've forked, and the program you're running is no longer what's globally accepted as Bitcoin. What you've just done is functionally equivalent to taking a photo of the Mona Lisa and claiming there are now two Mona Lisas. You can convince yourself that that's the case, but good luck convincing anyone else. We said that there was a kind of government in Bitcoin. That government is made up of every user that runs the software. The only way in which the protocol can be changed is if the majority of users agree on changes. Convincing a majority to add coins would be no easy task – after all, you're asking them to debase their own holdings. As it stands today, even seemingly insignificant features take years to reach consensus across the network. As it grows bigger in size, pushing changes will only get more difficult. Holders can, therefore, be reasonably confident that the supply won't be inflated. While the

software is man-made, the decentralization of the network means that Bitcoin acts more like a natural resource than code that can be arbitrarily changed.

The properties of good money

Believers in the store of value thesis also point to features of Bitcoin that make it good money. It's not just a scarce digital resource, but one that shares characteristics that have traditionally been adopted in currencies for centuries.

Gold has been used as money across civilizations since their inception. There are a handful of reasons for this. We've talked about durability and scarcity already. These can make good assets, but not necessarily good forms of currency. For that, you want fungibility, portability, and divisibility.

Fungibility

Fungibility means that units are indistinguishable. With gold, you can take any two ounces, and they'll be worth the same. This is true of things like stocks and cash as well. It doesn't matter which particular unit you're holding – it'll hold an equal value to any other of the same kind. Bitcoin fungibility is a tricky subject. It shouldn't really matter what coin you're holding. In most cases, 1 BTC = 1 BTC. Where it gets complicated is when you consider that each unit can be linked back to previous transactions. There are cases where businesses blacklist funds that they believe have been involved in criminal activities, even if the holder received them after. Should it matter? It's hard to see why. When you're paying for something with a dollar bill, neither you or the merchant know where it was used three-transactions ago. There's no concept of transaction history – new bills aren't worth more than used ones.

In a worst-case scenario, however, it's possible that the older bitcoins (with more history) are sold for less than newer bitcoins. Depending on who you ask, this scenario could be either the greatest threat to Bitcoin or not something to worry about. For now, anyway, Bitcoin is functionally fungible. There have only been isolated incidents of coins being frozen due to suspicious history.

Portability
Portability denotes the ease of transporting an asset. $10,000 in $100 bills? Easy enough to move around. $10,000 worth of oil? Not so much.
Good currency needs to have a small form factor. It needs to be easy to carry so that individuals can pay each other for goods and services.
Gold has traditionally been excellent in this regard. At the time of this writing, a standard gold coin holds almost $1,500 in value. It's unlikely that you'd be making purchases worth a full ounce of gold, so smaller denominations take up even less space.
Bitcoin is actually superior to precious metals when it comes to transportability. It doesn't even have a physical footprint. You could store trillions of dollars worth of wealth on a hardware device that fits in the palm of your hand. Moving one billion dollars of value in gold (over 20 tons currently) requires tremendous effort and expense. Even with cash, you would need to carry several pallets of $100 bills. With Bitcoin, you can send the same amount anywhere in the world for less than a dollar.

Divisibility
Another vital quality of currency is its divisibility – that is, the ability to split it into smaller units. With gold, you can take a one-ounce coin and cut it down the middle to produce two half-ounce units. You might lose a premium for destroying the nice drawing of an eagle or buffalo on it, but

the gold value remains the same. You can cut your half-ounce unit again and again to produce smaller denominations. Divisibility is another area where Bitcoin excels. There are only twenty-one million coins, but each one is made up of one-hundred million smaller units (satoshis). This gives users a great deal of control over their transactions, as they can specify an amount to send up to eight decimal places. Bitcoin's divisibility also makes it easier for small investors to buy fractions of BTC.

Store of Value, Medium of Exchange and Unit of Account

The sentiment is divided on Bitcoin's current role. Many believe that Bitcoin is simply a currency – a tool to move funds from point A to point B. We'll get into this in the next section, but this view is contrary to what many store of value proponents defend.

SoV proponents argue that Bitcoin must go through stages before it becomes the ultimate currency. It begins as a collectible (arguably where we are now): it has proven itself as functional and secure but has only been adopted by a small niche. Its core audience consists primarily of hobbyists and speculators.

Only once there is greater education, infrastructure for institutions, and more confidence in its capability to retain value can it progress to the next stage: store of value. Some believe it has already reached this level.

At this point, Bitcoin isn't widely spent due to Gresham's law, which states that bad money drives out good money. What this means is that, when presented with two kinds of currency, individuals will be inclined to spend the inferior one and to hoard the superior one. Users of Bitcoin prefer to spend fiat currencies, as they have little faith in their long-term survival. They hold (or HODL) their bitcoins, as they believe that they'll retain value.

If the Bitcoin network continues to grow, more users will adopt it, liquidity will increase, and the price will become more stable. Because of stronger stability, there won't be as much of an incentive to hold it in hopes of higher gains in the future. So we could expect it to be used a lot more in commerce and daily payments, as a strong medium of exchange. Increased usage further stabilizes the price. In the final stage, Bitcoin would become a unit of account – it would be used to price other assets. Just as you might price a gallon of oil at $4, a world where Bitcoin reigns as money would have you measuring its value in bitcoins. If these three monetary milestones are achieved, proponents see a future where Bitcoin has become a new standard that displaces the currencies used today.

The case against Bitcoin as a store of value

The arguments presented in the previous section may sound completely logical to some and like insanity to others. There are a handful of criticisms of the idea of Bitcoin as "digital gold," coming both from Bitcoiners and from cryptocurrency skeptics.

Bitcoin as digital cash

Many are quick to point to the Bitcoin white paper when a disagreement on the topic arises. To them, it's apparent that Satoshi intended for Bitcoin to be spent from the get-go. In fact, it's in the very title of the paper: Bitcoin: A Peer-to-Peer Electronic Cash System. The argument suggests that Bitcoin can only be valuable if users spend their coins. By hoarding them, you're not aiding adoption – you're harming it. If Bitcoin isn't widely appreciated as digital cash, its core proposition is driven not by utility, but by speculation. These ideological differences led to a significant fork in 2017. The minority of Bitcoiners wanted a system with bigger blocks, which meant cheaper transaction fees. Due to increased usage of the original network, the cost of a transaction could rise dramatically, and price many users out of lower-value transactions. If there's an average fee of $10, it makes little sense for you to spend coins on a $3 purchase. The forked network is known now as Bitcoin Cash. The original network rolled out its own upgrade around the time, known as SegWit. SegWit did nominally increase the capacity of the blocks, but that was not its main goal. It also laid the groundwork for the Lightning Network, which seeks to facilitate low-fee transactions by pushing them off-chain. In practice, however, the Lightning Network is far from perfect. Regular Bitcoin transactions are considerably easier to understand, whereas managing Lightning Network channels and capacity comes with a steep learning curve. It remains to be seen whether it can be streamlined, or whether the solution's design is fundamentally too complex to abstract away. Because of the rising demand for block space, on-chain transactions are no longer as cheap at busy times. As such, one could put forward the argument that not increasing the block size damages Bitcoin's usability as currency.

No intrinsic value
To many, the comparison between gold and Bitcoin is absurd. The history of gold is, essentially, the history of civilization. The precious metal has been a critical part of societies for thousands of years. Admittedly, it's lost some of its dominance since the eradication of the gold standard but nonetheless remains the quintessential safe-haven asset. Indeed, it does seem like a stretch to compare the network effects of the king of assets to an eleven-year-old protocol. Gold has been revered both as a status symbol and as an industrial metal for millennia. In contrast, Bitcoin has no use outside of its network. You can't use it as a conductor in electronics, nor can you craft it into a massive shiny chain

when you decide to launch a hip-hop career. It may emulate gold (mining, finite supply, etc.), but that doesn't change the fact that it's a digital asset. To an extent, all money is a shared belief – the dollar only has value because the government says so and society accepts it. Gold only has value because everyone agrees that it does. Bitcoin isn't any different, but those that give it value are still a tiny group in the grand scheme. You've likely had many conversations in your personal life where you've had to explain what it is because the vast majority of people are unaware of it.

Volatility and correlation
Those that got into Bitcoin early have certainly enjoyed their wealth growing by orders of magnitude. To them, it has indeed stored value – and then some. But those that purchased their first coins at all-time high have no such experience. Many had big losses by selling at any point afterward. Bitcoin is incredibly volatile, and its markets are unpredictable. Metals like gold and silver have insignificant fluctuations in comparison. You could make the case that it's too early, and that the price will eventually stabilize. But that, in itself, could point to Bitcoin not currently being a store of value. There's also Bitcoin's relation to traditional markets to consider. Since Bitcoin's inception, they've been on a steady uptrend. The cryptocurrency hasn't truly been tested as a safe-haven asset if all other asset classes are also doing well. Bitcoin enthusiasts might refer to it as "uncorrelated" with other assets, but there's just no way of knowing that until other assets suffer while Bitcoin remains steady.

Tulip Mania and Beanie Babies
It wouldn't be a proper criticism of Bitcoin's store of value properties if we didn't bring up the comparisons to Tulip Mania and Beanie Babies. These are weak analogies at the best of times, but they serve to illustrate the dangers of a bursting bubble. In both instances, investors flocked to buy items that they perceived to be rare in the hopes of reselling them for a profit. In and of themselves, the items weren't that valuable – they were relatively easy to produce. The bubble popped when investors realized that they were overvaluing their investments massively, and the markets for tulips and Beanie babies subsequently collapsed. Again, these are weak analogies. Bitcoin's value does stem from users' belief in it but, unlike tulips, more cannot be grown to satisfy demand. That said, nothing guarantees that investors won't see Bitcoin as overvalued in the future, causing its own bubble to burst.

Closing thoughts
Bitcoin certainly shares most of the features of a store of value like gold. The number of units is finite, the network is decentralized enough to offer security to holders, and it can be used to hold and transfer value. Ultimately, it must still prove its worth as a safe-haven asset – it's too early to say for sure. Things could go both ways – the world may flee to Bitcoin in times of economic turmoil, or it could continue to be used only by a minority group.

CHAPTER SEVEN
HOW TO BUILD A MINING RIG: THINGS YOU NEED TO KNOW BEFORE YOU START

If you liked playing archeologist-types of games when you were a kid and DIY videos are a usual sight in your YouTube playlist, then you have come to the right place. Today I'm going to tell you about all of the different ways on how to build a mining rig. Mining rigs might seem tricky at first, but when you break them down, it's not that hard. In this guide, we'll cover some of the basic things about mining rigs: their components (and what are the best component manufacturers), how they work, best placement ideas and so on. We'll start with the definitions and then work our way from there.

Types of Mining Rigs

• CPU. CPU mining rigs utilize processors to "mine" data from the blockchain. These are very simple and inexpensive rigs – most people, when they talk about CPU mining, mean that they mine cryptocurrencies straight from their computer. This has its benefits and drawbacks (having much more of the latter). CPU mining is becoming more and more unpopular as the years go by. There are many contributors to the reasoning behind this, however, one of the bigger ones is the price. CPU mining is very costly and clunky – your electricity bills are going to skyrocket through the roof, while your computer might overheat at any given second if you lack proper cooling. The main perk that the CPU method of mining has is its availability. You could download a few programs (more on them later) to your desktop or laptop (although using laptops for mining cryptos is strongly unadvised) and start mining right this instant. People who don't want to invest a lot (or any) of money favor CPU mining because it requires zero effort.

• GPU. GPU cryptocurrency mining rigs are the absolute favorites for people looking at how to build a mining rig. They're definitely among the most popular crypto farming methods out there – anyone from a single miner to a corporation, possessing a whole mining farm, tend to use GPU rigs. GPU mining rigs utilize graphics card GPUs to mine data from the blockchain. They can be dedicated or simple miners – dedicated GPU mining rigs are built for a solemn purpose of cryptocurrency mining, while simple miners are devices that are used for other intents and purposes, doing crypto mining only on the side (i.e. desktop computers). People love GPU mining rigs for their usefulness – these rigs do the job and they do it with grace. Naturally, to get the best results, you would have to use the maximum amount of GPUs available, but even with the simplest of rigs, a result would be noticeable.GPU mining rigs do have a couple of downsides, however, that a person looking on how to build a mining rig should know. The biggest downside is its price. Graphics cards tend to be quite expensive (or very expensive, if you're aiming for the best of the best), so the initial investment you might have to make could be somewhat significant. They also require maintenance – a lot of cooling, plenty of electricity to fuel their power, generally looking after and taking care of, etc.

• ASIC. ASICs, or Application-Specific Integrated Circuits, are special devices designed explicitly with one, designated purpose in mind. These devices are the current top-dogs when it comes to cryptocurrency mining rigs. Someone who's looking for how to build a mining rig should know that, while not being rigs per say, ASICs are pieces of dedicated machinery that you can purchase and set up so it would mine cryptos for you. They are very popular, which in turn makes them extremely scarce to come by. If making money through cryptocurrencies is your only objective, then ASICs are a perfect choice. However, if you care about the ecosystem that is the crypto world, you might want to think twice. Because of how powerful they are, ASICs have a reputation of twisting the wellbeing of cryptocurrencies and throwing miners that use other types of rigs out of balance. Because of these reasons, ASICs have recently been subject to a high level of controversy that sparked within the Ethereum mining community and continues to echo through ought the crypto world.

These were the three types of the most commonly used mining rigs out there. Although the information may vary, the most popular out of the three stems to be the GPU type, with ASIC and CPU ones as follow-ups, respectively.

Now that you have a general understanding of the main types of mining rigs, their pros and cons, we can move on to the main topic at hand – how to build a mining rig.

How to Build a Mining Rig?

Let's just say that when you're thinking about how to build a mining rig, you're thinking about a GPU one. ASICs are devices on their own (they require no initial building from your part), while CPU rigs are built in the same way as the GPU one, with their main component being the one differentiator.

Things to Keep in Mind

So how to build a mining rig? Well, first of all, you have to know what to take into consideration when picking the parts for your rig.

Naturally, there are quite a few things to keep in mind, but the main ones would probably have to be hash rate and energy consumption.

Hash rate defines just how powerful your rig is. It's a way of knowing how many calculations your rig can perform in one second. The higher the amount, the better. Naturally, though, high hash rates mean high demand for power, which in turn results in a high electricity bill. For anyone thinking about how to build a mining rig, this should be a big factor to take into consideration.

Energy consumption is another major factor to consider when thinking about how to build a mining rig, and one people tend to disregard it. You should never let the illusion that "I bought my mining rig components, which means I'm done spending" get in your head. Mining energy costs might not only match your profits but even exceed them and leave you completely broke and in debt.

When choosing your hardware, always try to strike a perfect balance between the power of a component, and the power consumption.

Finally, don't just jump into the first market site and buy everything that pops up on your screen when you Google "best hardware for building a mining rig". With a little bit of digging, you might find the same components for a lot cheaper. Be smart – cryptocurrency mining is a competitive business, so every dollar counts!

Components

Let's make a quick overview of the components that you'll need for building a mining rig.

Generally, what you're going to look for are the following parts:

• Motherboard. This is one of the main components of your rig. Generally, a motherboard determines the rest of your components in the rig (or, in other words, determines the compatibility of the rig). When choosing a motherboard, if it's the first item you're looking for, always check the graphics cards that it works well with.

• Graphics card(s). The GPUs are an essential part of your rig. They determine whether your mining rig is going to be top-notch, or meh. The two main companies producing and selling top-tier graphics cards are Nvidia and AMD. When you pick your cards, remember to check online if they're suitable for cryptocurrency mining. Remember, though, that a good rig has to be made out of several or more GPUs – plan your funds and other purchases accordingly when thinking how to build a mining rig.

• Power supply. The power supply that you'll have to get depends solemnly on the other components of your rig. If you're trying to build a hardcore, supercharged cryptocurrency mining rig, then the power supply is going to have to match that. In most cases, though, a medium level power supply does the job perfectly.

• Cooling. A very important factor in any type of mining rig, cooling is going to ensure that your device works properly and prevent any type of possible overheating. Don't be cheap and invest in the best cooling possible – it's always better to be safe than sorry.

• CPU. A good processor is going to be key when it comes to being able to run the rig smoothly and without any major faults or errors.

• Frame. A mining rig frame is the last key component that you'll need (at least when it comes to GPU mining rigs). A mining rig frame is going to be the carcass of your device – these frames come in a wide variety of choices, and it's preferential. Naturally, though, you're probably going to want to use something sturdy and will hold the whole machine together, rather than a frame that'll break from the first piece of dust that falls on to it.

With all of the parts acquired, let's move on to the building process itself.

The Building Process

To be frank, the building process itself is quite straightforward. Let's talk about how to build a mining rig.

The very first step that you'll need to take is to set up the motherboard inside of the mining rig frame. Building a mining rig becomes that much easier when you've already picked a suitable spot for the rig to stay in, though, so pick a good spot in advance.

After you've set up the motherboard, plug the cables into the CPU. Set up the graphics cards and the rest of the needed hardware and plug the cables in, respectively.

Now that you've got the hardware in place, double-check the cable placement and if all's well in place, it's time to move on to the software. Depending on the software you've chosen, your rig might have a few fancier functions, or be completely basic. Fancy doesn't always equate to good, though, so pick a secure software, has a good reputation and works well. The online crypto forums are a good place to look for and review cryptocurrency mining software. When thinking about how to build a mining rig, software shouldn't be excluded from the picture – good software is often what makes it or breaks it. After installing the software, configure the options to your liking and proceed with the setup. Your device will have to reboot a few times before it's fully operational, so be patient. After all of this is done, you can officially begin your career as a professional cryptocurrency miner!

Each of the hundreds of crypto coins in existence rely on the core concept of the blockchain. Cryptocurrency was designed to be decentralized, secure and unalterable. So every single transaction is encrypted. Once that encrypted transaction happens it's added to something called a "block" until a fixed number of transactions has been recorded. That block then gets added to a chain -- the blockchain -- which is publicly available.

These transactions leave no trace of who is behind them, however, because privacy is also a pillar of cryptocurrency. The location of the transactions isn't centralized, either, so that it can't be manipulated or controlled by one person or entity. Since these blocks are heavily encrypted, they're sort of like complicated math puzzles that only powerful compute-capable hardware can solve. Enter your CPU, or your Radeon and GeForce graphics cards. The process of solving the math puzzles on these blocks and adding them to the public blockchain (think of it as a ledger) is roughy what mining is.

Miners verify the transactions, ensure they aren't false, and keep the infrastructure humming along.

The reward for doing so -- a miner's fee if you will -- is payment in that block's coin. The payment is based on how much their hardware contributed to solving that puzzle. Where do the coins come from? By design, that's exactly how the coins are created. The block is solved and coins and distributed fairly to miners. This increases the coin's supply.

The Best Analogy: Google Docs

In 2016 William Mougayar wrote a brilliant piece explaining blockchain technology by leveraging something we all know about: word processing programs. He reminds us that when Microsoft Word was the only game in town, one person had to create a file, open it, then send it to another person to have it edited or updated. The similarity to banks is striking, and makes it clear why blockchain technology was created in the first place: That's how databases work today. Two owners can't update the same record at once. That's how banks maintain money balances and transfers; they briefly lock access (or decrease the balance) while they make a transfer, then update the other side, then reopen access (or update again).

With Google Docs (or Google Sheets), both parties have access to the same document at the same time, and the single version of that document is always visible to both of them. It is like a shared ledger, but it is a shared document. The distributed part comes into play when sharing involves a number of people.

Imagine the number of legal documents that should be used that way. ~William Mougayar

The cool thing is that blockchain technology can be used for much more than financial transactions. It was designed to not have a single point of failure, and to be fully transparent. That's why you see it rapidly emerging in the gaming space, too. It can be utilized for secure cloud storage distributed across thousands of computers. Physical objects could conceivably be given unique digital ownership or identities. Anything of value can be integrated with blockchain technology. The possibilities at this point are endless and reliant on the imaginations of developers.

The Basics of Cryptocurrency Mining

We'll dive deeper into this in the future, but the elements that go into mining on your computer involve specialized or consumer hardware and a combination of your graphics cards and CPU. The most efficient mining apps still seem to be command-line based, but there are some elegant ones with traditional graphics interfaces. In your journey you may stumble across names like ccminer, Claymore or XMR-Stak. You'll download the software you need to mine a specific coin and edit an executable text file with details like the mining pool's URL to connect to, your wallet address and the name of your "worker" or PC. More advanced options allow you to adjust how hard your GPU or CPU works. The vast majority of this software works across Windows and Linux, although it's more difficult to configure on non-Windows systems. What makes it more challenging is that these variables are formatted differently depending on the pools and the software.

Once the blocks I mentioned above are solved and coins are generated, the pool automatically pays the miners directly to their wallet, or to an online cryptocurrency exchange that holds many different types of coins. I understand that this is simplifying things to the extreme, but that's why an entire series of guides is needed! It's a complex landscape to understand, but the core is simple: miners are people independently verifying transactions on the coin's network, and when that happens more coins are created. Miners effectively keep the network running and increase the coin's global supply. Some mine to engage in a unique kind of hobby, or for sheer profit. Others do it because they believe in the principles behind a certain coin and in what the developers intend to do with it. The reasons you have are yours, but I'll try to guide you through it.

Conclusion

As more and more people turn towards cryptocurrencies, there's a vast increase in a need for experts in the field. People who have a comprehension of how to build their mining rigs are quite far ahead in the crypto department – after all, you don't only learn about the rig itself, but about the software needed, how cryptos work, how to use the market, etc.

At this point, you should be at least somewhat knowledgeable on the topics of crypto mining rig hardware and software, how to choose certain specific items, what criteria to look at and what to ignore, how to assemble the rig itself, etc. Be sure to put this knowledge to good use, and remember – Rome wasn't built in a day. It takes a lot of practice to build a pristine mining rig, so don't stress if it doesn't work out for the first couple of times.

And remember, it's always better to be safe than sorry. Choose the right equipment for the job, both from the hardware and the software standpoints. Don't hesitate to invest in something that will not only do the job for you but will keep your funds secure and last for a long time, rather than breaking apart in the first couple of months. Decent equipment can do wonders – just don't be afraid to experiment!

CONCLUSION

The big question of how to get bitcoins.

After acquiring a basic knowledge of what bitcoin is and how the wallet really work, you may want to get into the digital currency world and get some bitcoin for yourself. Thus the big question arrives to your mind: How do I get bitcoins?After you get the knowledge of the origin of every single bitcoin, which is based on a mining process, you'll believe that the best way to get them is by joining this mining process. The thing is that, this has become very difficult, because the fast popularity grow of the crypto currency.

Sell products or services.
Every single bitcoin comes as the result of a previous transaction. Thus, the way to get them, when you don't have any, is by receiving a transaction from someone else, when you purchase them using cash or also by mining new bitcoins. When you know an individual, who uses bitcoins, you can ask him/her to get bitcoins. In case you don't know anyone who posses them, you can get bitcoins by offering another kind of transaction with just another bitcoin user,

resulting you getting paid in bitcoins. The alternative option is by mining them yourself.

Mining.
In case you cannot purchase bitcoin from someone else, you can get them by mining them. The term mining here means: solving a complex mathematical problem, which intention is to validate other individuals transactions. In return you're awarded with bitcoins. Receiving bitcoins is sometimes free, but a fee may be included for sending them, it depends on the online platform you use. Before getting into mining bitcoins, you need to understand, that it's not an easy way to get bitcoins, it requires some tech knowledge, which may not be practical for you.

Buy.
In case, you don't know anyone who posses bitcoins, you don't have anything to sell to exchange for bitcoins, there's a way to buy bitcoins. There're several online platforms, these sell bitcoins by a process called trading/exchanging. Here I list some ways you can purchase bitcoins:

Buy bitcoins from a person.
There are online marketplaces where you can buy bitcoins in a person-to-person scheme. You can pay these individuals with cash or by other ways. The good think is that you and the seller can arrange the payment method: cash in person, cash by deposit, bank wire, PayPal, etc. The key element here is to find someone trustworthy. A good tip is using an escrow online service, this way you can protect yourself against any kind of fraud. The good thing about these online escrow platform, is that everyone should upload their scanned ID, this guarantees security during the transactions.

Buy bitcoins from an exchange and outlet.
Bitcoin exchanges or outlets are basically online services that make it easier for buyers and seller to do bitcoins transactions. To be part of one of these, all you need is to create an account and get your identity verification before you can buy or sell bitcoins.

Buy bitcoins through an ATM.
Some cities around the world offer physical bitcoin ATMs. You just get your bitcoins through them using local fiat currency. Governments regulate the uses of these ATMs for security purposes. Sometimes finding a bitcoin ATM near your location may be difficult, because even the location where these are installed is regulated.

www.ingramcontent.com/pod-product-compliance
Lightning Source LLC
Chambersburg PA
CBHW071127240526
45465CB00024B/1474